STUDENT GUIDE

to accompany

MARRIAGE IN A CHANGING WORLD, 2nd EDITION

John C. Touhey

Florida Atlantic University

John Wiley & Sons

New York · Chichester · Brisbane · Toronto

INTRODUCTION

Each chapter of the <u>Student Guide</u> to accompany <u>Marriage in a Changing World</u> corresponds to a chapter in the text, and it provides several exercises that alert you to the materials which require further review. By rereading the relevant parts of the text, you may then clear up these areas of difficulty. Each chapter of the Student Guide contains the following parts:

<u>Key Terms and Concepts</u>: A list of major terms and ideas for you to review. If you can correctly identify each of these words, you will have a good overview of the material.

<u>Learning Objectives</u>: A series of sentence completions covering the essential concepts and information in each chapter. This material closely tied in to the text.

<u>Multiple-Choice, True-False, and Matching Questions</u>: A series of questions designed to test your recall of important concepts, ideas, and findings. These questions also give you an idea of what you eventually may be tested on by your instructor.

<u>Essay Questions</u>: These questions provide an opportunity for you to probe and describe in detail several key points made in the book. Here you test not only your recall, but your ability to analyze a problem.

<u>Answers</u>: Solutions to all objective questions appear at the end of each chapter. We hope these exercises will contribute to a worthwhile learning experience.

TABLE OF CONTENTS

Introduction

Chapter 1

LIFE IN MODERN SOCIETY

KEY TERMS AND CONCEPTS

Human Values: The fundamental beliefs and customs that state the worth of what is human and which transcend the divisions of sex, class, race, ethnic origin, and nationality.

Individual Worth: The welfare of each individual is a goal of high priority and the welfare of the whole of human kind is linked with the welfare of individuals.

Interpersonal Intimacy: Loving relationships provide individuals with a sense of their own significance and nurture that sense. Early associations provide the basis for future relationships. The need for interpersonal intimacy continues throughout life.

Personal Growth and Development: The awareness of that worth fostered in loving relationships, and each person has a responsibility to become healthy and creative and to participate only in relationships that support personal growth.

Responsibility for the Welfare of Others: Early associations provide the security and trust necessary for emotionally supportive relationships.

Likelihood of Marriage: The currently married amount to close to three-fourths of the adult population, and approximately 95% of the population will eventually marry.

Singlehood: A new stereotype of swinging singles reflects the lifestyle of only a privileged few. The majority of singles differ little in social or personality characteristics from their married counterparts.

Problems of Singles Living: Singles housing and recreational facilities cater only to the young and affluent. Sexual relationships require excessive time or the individual suffers frequent loneliness.

Frequent Divorce: The absolute number and the rate of divorce approximately doubled in the decade from 1965 through 1974. One-fourth to one-third of the 30-year-old people currently married will divorce.

1

<u>Remarriage</u>: Remarriage rates are not rising as rapidly as divorce rates. Men are more likely to remarry than women.

<u>Group Marriage</u>: The most popular arrangement is based on two couples who decide to form a common household. Love and sharing is fostered, and sex role stereotyping is reduced. Financial advantages are obvious, but the marriages are vulnerable to disruption.

<u>Communal Living</u>: Communes contain from a few people to a hundred or more. There is a high turnover of members. Ownership of private property is avoided and self-sufficiency is striven for. Many communes are close to campuses and the age of their members reflects this. The typical self-sufficient commune is rural with an agricultural base.

<u>Inevitability of Widowhood</u>: The fact that women outlive men by about eight years together with the practice of marrying men three years older ordains that they will spend a decade alone. There are five times as many widows as widowers, and the remarriage rate for widowers is five times that of widows.

<u>Future Marriage and Family Relationships</u>: There will be a greater range of alternatives. People will be free to remain single with or without sexual or living arrangements; harassment of homosexuals will decrease; multiple-person arrangements will be a way of life for some; there will be freedom to have or not have children; unrewarding marriages will be concluded; spouses will be encouraged to grow as persons; and children will be planned for and welcomed.

LEARNING OBJECTIVES

Fill in the words required to complete each sentence.

Learning Objective 1

Describe the basic family values of the western world.

a. Despite rapid _change_ in modern marriage practices, many scholars contend that basic family values are simply being _expressed_ under new _circumstances_

b. One basic family value emphasizes the _worth_ of the individual, and that social change must be judged by its impact on the _welfare_ of the individual.

c. A second basic value states that _intimacy_ results from loving interpersonal _relations_. For most adults, intimate _heterosexual_ relationships are the major sources of one's feelings of _self worth_.

d. Another basic family value is the evaluation of _RElATioNShips_ in terms of their capacity to promote personal _gROWTh_ and _Development_ Most recently it has been emphasized that _mARRied_ should permit the continued _personal_ growth of both husband and wife.

e. People first learn to _Love_ others in relationships with _fAmily_, relatives, and friends. Later, the process of loving others leads most adults to _mARRiage_ and _pARENThooD_.

Learning Objective 2

Explain how basic family values have endured in new settings.

a. While it is now easier for people to remain _SiNgle_, people of both _Sexs_ are more likely to _mARRy_ than ever before.

b. The proportion of the United States population who ever marry is approximately _95%_ percent, and about _75%_ percent of our adult population is presently married.

c. The traditional stereotype of unmarried people as lonely _losers_ has yielded to the new stereotype of _swiNgiNg_ singles.

d. The proportion of _youNg_ unmarried adults has _iNcReAsed_ since 1960. The _mediAN_ age of first marriage has also risen more than _oNe_ year(s) since 1960.

e. _DemogRApheRs_ have referred to the temporary recent surplus of marriageable _womeN_ as the "marriage squeeze." But as the surplus of marriageable women _decReAses_, the trend toward _siNglehood_ may also decline.

f. The proportion of the population over the age of _30_ remaining single has _dRopped_ since 1960.

g. Most singles' apartments and bars are rigidly segregated by _Age_ and _ecoNomic_ status.

h. Singles must either devote inordinate resources to developing _heteroSexual_ relationships, or they experience frequent _loNliness_.

Learning Objective 3

Describe the basic characteristics of divorce in the United States.

a. From 1966 to 1976, the number of divorces has more than _douBled_ to over _oNe_ million per year. The divorce _RATe_ increased during

4

the same period from 2.5 to 4.7 per ___1000___ population per year.

b. About one-third of all ___30___ -year-old married people will eventually _divorce_ . About ___3/4___ of these divorced people will _remarry_ .

c. The divorce ___RATE___ of 50 years ago was about ___1/3___ of today's rate.

d. Most _Remarried_ people describe themselves and their ___children___ as being better off than before. Divorce is often a necessary step in the ___growth___ of two people toward greater social and ___MATurity___ maturity.

e. The recent drop in the _Remarried_ rate probably means that more divorced people ___Living___ with their new partners before remarrying. Due to women's greater ___survival___ , divorced men are about ___TWO___ times more likely to ___Remarry___ than are divorced women.

Learning Objective 4

Describe the basic characteristics of group marriage in the United States.

a. Only a few ___thousand___ people are presently involved in group marriage, but many who have not tried group marriage consider it as a _possiblity_ .

b. The most common group marriage ___ARANgment___ involves ___2___ married couples. Frequently one or both couples are _dissatisfied_ with their own ___Marrige___ .

c. Most group marriage members are committed to ideals of ___INtamacy___ they find difficult to realize in _convetional_ marriages. Most groups use such techniques as ___dissussion___ and ___MUTUAl___ criticism to eliminate defensiveness.

d. ___Sexual___ sharing in group marriage is part of a more ___general___ sharing of resources. Two additional advantages claimed for group marriage are reduced living ___costs___ and better _child-Rearing_ practices.

e. Since group marriages are not ___legally___ sanctioned, formal _divorces_ are not required in order to end them. Yet group marriages are ___more___ likely than _convetional_ marriages to break up.

f. Group marriage is usually only a _temporary_ part of youths' search for fulfilling interpersonal _Relationships_

Learning Objective 5

Describe the principal features of communal living in the United States.

a. As many as ___3000___ communes have been started in recent years. Some communes have emphasized ___DRUG___ use, while others have emphasized ___FiNACIAl___ advantage, and others have included married couples living ___MONOGAMMY___.

b. Other common characteristics of communes include abolition of private ___property___, ___economic___ self-sufficiency, disavowal of conventional ___sex___ roles, and sharing of all productive ___tasks___.

c. Most people try communal living in their late ___teens___ or early ___twenties___, and many communes are located near ___colleges___. Most ___universitys___ communal living seldom lasts beyond the ___college___ years.

d. The typical ___selfsuficet___ commune is rural and ___Agriculturaly___ based. Most communes do not ___survive___ for more than a ___few___ years, and most ex-members seem to disappear into the larger ___society___.

Learning Objective 6

Describe recent developments in the understanding of widowhood.

a. Death of one's ___spouse___ is hardly a recent development, but society has moved toward a new ___awanness___ of widowhood.

b. Women ___survive___ men by an average of nearly ___8___ years, and the average wife is two to three years ___younger___ than her husband.

c. Among persons over the age of 65, about ___80___ percent of the men have wives, but only ___40___ percent of the women have husbands.

d. Women who are widowed will live for an average of ___10___ additional years.

e. The ___remarriage___ rate for widowers is about ___4___ times greater than that of widows.

f. The prospect of widowhood seems quite ___unreal___ to most ___young___ people. Thus, mate ___selection___, career ___preparation___, and financial planning seldom take account of widowhood.

6

Learning Objective 7

Describe the most likely characteristics of marriage and family in the future.

a. Some examples of wide choices will include the right to remain _Single_ , and _homosexuality_ will be freer from social harassment.

b. Fewer marriages will produce _Children_ , and many couples will focus exclusively on their personal and _pair_ growth.

c. High rates of divorce may produce better _remarriages_ . Marital permanence will depend on the extent to which each marriage meets the _emotional_ , intellectual, and _physical_ needs of both partners.

d. There will be more emphasis on husbands and wives as _persons_ apart from their marital _Roles_ .

e. Children will more often be planned and consciously _desired_ , and they will become more _Authentic_ persons.

MULTIPLE CHOICE QUESTIONS

_b_ 1. Which of the following is <u>not</u> one of the basic family values of the western world?

    a. worth of the individual
    b. heterosexual gratification
    c. intimacy in interpersonal relations
    d. personal growth and development

_A_ 2. There are presently about _____ million American couples living together without being married?

    a. one   c. four
    b. two   d. eight

_d_ 3. Approximately _____ percent of all Americans will marry at least one time.

    a. 65   c. 85
    b. 75   d. 95

_C_ 4. The old stereotype of unmarried adults as "lonely losers" has yielded to the new media stereotype of

    a. cohabiting couples.

    b.   promiscuous pairs.
    c.   swinging singles.
    d.   parents without partners.

B 5. With respect to the emergence of a new life style of permanent singlehood, the latest research findings suggest that

    a.   more younger adults are marrying, while more older adults remain single.
    b.   more younger adults are remaining single, while more older adults marry.
    c.   adults of all ages are more likely to marry.
    d.   adults of all ages are less likely to marry.

C 6. Studies which compare the personality and social characteristics of married and single people show

    a.   that married people are happier and better adjusted.
    b.   that single people are happier and better adjusted.
    c.   few differences between each group.
    d.   that single people are happier, while married people are better adjusted.

B 7. Compared to 1967, the United States divorce rate in 1977 had

    a.   remained constant.
    b.   nearly doubled.
    c.   nearly tripled.
    d.   dropped about 20 percent.

A 8. Divorced people who have remarried most often describe themselves as

    a.   happier than in their previous marriage.
    b.   less happy than in their previous marriage.
    c.   about as happy as in their previous marriage.
    d.   less happy than in the period between marriages.

b 9. Divorce is often a necessary step in the individual's growth toward increased

    a.   occupational and financial success.
    b.   social and emotional maturity.
    c.   sexual gratification.
    d.   religious participation.

A 10. Rates of remarriage are

    a.   higher for men than for women.
    b.   higher for women than for men.
    c.   approximately the same for each sex.
    d.   higher for widows than for widowers.

__C__ 11. The most common group marriage arrangement in the United States involves

    a. a man and two women.
    b. a woman and two men.
    c. two couples.
    d. several couples.

__D__ 12. Which of the following is <u>least</u> characteristic of communal living in the United States?

    a. renunciation of private property
    b. abolition of sex roles
    c. efforts toward economic self-sufficiency
    d. mandatory religious participation

__C__ 13. The average woman who is widowed can expect to live for another _____ years.

    a. two   c. ten
    b. six   d. fourteen

__A__ 14. There are about _____ as many widowers as widows in the United States.

    a. one-fourth   c. three-fourths
    b. one-half   d. twice

__D__ 15. About 50% of all marriages reach their _____ wedding anniversary.

    a. 20th   c. 30th
    b. 25th   d. 35th

__D__ 16. Given the continuation of present trends, marriages in the future will probably be characterized by

    a. a narrower range of choices.
    b. lower divorce rates.
    c. more emphasis on husbands and wives fulfilling their marital roles.
    d. more consciously chosen child-bearing.

TRUE FALSE QUESTIONS

__F__ 1. In a period of rapid social change, only marriage and family life can be expected to remain the same.

___T___ 2. Worth of the individual is one of the basic family values of the western world.

___T___ 3. About 80 percent of those who divorce will eventually remarry.

___F___ 4. The proportion of young married adults in the United States has increased since 1960.

___T___ 5. Median age at first marriage has increased since 1965.

___T___ 6. Singles' apartments and bars are usually segregated by age and economic status.

___F___ 7. Single living is most preferred by low income workers who live in rural settings.

___F___ 8. Most remarried people describe themselves as less happy than in their previous marriage.

___T___ 9. Remarriage rates are higher for divorced men than for divorced women.

___F___ 10. Group marriages are less likely to break up than conventional marriages.

___F___ 11. The modern self-sufficient commune is typically urban and involved in industrial production.

___T___ 12. High rates of divorce appear to produce more satisfactory marriages.

MATCHING

___D___ 1. basic family values

___F___ 2. single people

___G___ 3. divorce

___A___ 4. remarriage

___B___ 5. group marriage

___C___ 6. communal living

___H___ 7. widowhood

___E___ 8. future marriage

a. more likely for men

b. typically involves two couples

c. self-sufficient and agricultural

d. worth, intimacy, growth, and responsibility

e. greater choice, variation, and loving environment

f. similar to married people

g. over two million per year

h. more likely for women

ESSAY QUESTIONS

1. Explain why the success of marriage is increasingly evaluated in terms of personal gratification rather than marital role performance. How have recent social trends contributed to this change?

2. Explain why increasing numbers of married couples are choosing to remain childless and relate your answer to the changing social conditions of urban and suburban life.

3. Discuss the advantages and limitations of permanent singlehood as a new life style. How do singles deal with such problems as loneliness, unemployment, and sickness?

ANSWERS

Learning Objective 1

a. change, expressed, circumstances
b. worth, welfare
c. intimacy, relations, heterosexual, self-worth
d. relationships, growth, development, marriage, personal
e. love, parents, marriage, parenthood

Learning Objective 2

a. single, sexes, marry
b. 95, 75
c. losers, swinging
d. young, increased, median, one
e. demographers, women, squeeze, decreases, singlehood
f. 30, decreased
g. age, economic
h. heterosexual, loneliness

Learning Objective 3

a. doubled, one, rate, 1000
b. 30, divorce, three-fourths, remarry
c. rate, one-third
d. remarried, children, growth, emotional
e. remarriage, live, survival, two, remarry

Learning Objective 4

a. thousand, possibility
b. arrangement, two, dissatisfied, marriage
c. intimacy, conventional, discussion, mutual
d. sexual, general, expense, child-rearing
e. legally, divorces, more, conventional
f. temporary, relationships

Learning Objective 5

a. 3000, drug, financial, monogamously
b. property, economic, sex, tasks
c. teens, twenties, universities, college

d. self-sufficient, agriculturally, survive, few, society

Learning Objective 6

a. spouse, awareness
b. outlive, eight, younger
c. 80, 40
d. ten
e. remarriage, four
f. unreal, young, selection, preparation

Learning Objective 7

a. single, homosexuals
b. children, pair
c. marriages, emotional, physical
d. persons, roles
e. desired, authentic

MULTIPLE CHOICE QUESTIONS

1. b   9. b
2. a   10. a
3. d   11. c
4. c   12. d
5. b   13. c
6. c   14. a
7. b   15. d
8. a   16. d

TRUE FALSE QUESTIONS

1. F   7. F
2. T   8. F
3. T   9. T
4. F   10. F
5. T   11. F
6. T   12. T

MATCHING

1. d
2. f
3. g
4. a
5. b
6. c
7. h
8. e

Chapter 2

PERSONALITY PREPARATION FOR PAIR LIVING

KEY TERMS AND CONCEPTS

Primary Sex Ratio: The number of males per 100 females at the time of conception.

Secondary Sex Ratio: The number of males per 100 females at the time of birth.

Tertiary Sex Ratio: The number of males per 100 females at adulthood.

Chromosomal Sexual Abnormalities: The loss or gain of sex chromosomes during cell division which may cause adjustment problems.

Intrauterine Influences: The chemical balance, mostly hormonal, within the uterus during the time the embryo develops.

Progestins: Substitutes for the pregnancy hormone progesterone prescribed during the 1950s to prevent miscarriages.

Hermaphroditic Characteristics: Having sexual organs of both sexes. In the case of the progestin-masculinized female fetuses and the androgenital syndrome female fetuses, internal organs were female and external organs were masculine to varying degress.

Progestin-Induced Hermaphrodites: Fetuses who were chromosomal females subjected to masculinizing hormones while developing in the uterus. Their external sexual organs were masculine to varying degress and they required corrective surgery.

Androgenital Syndrome: A malfunction of the adrenal glands resulting in the failure to produce the hormone cortisol and the production of a hormone similar to the male androgen. It affects chromosomal female fetuses by masculinizing their external sexual organs to varying degrees. Beyond corrective surgery, the female requires continuing cortisone therapy.

Brain Circuitry Influences: Some scientists believe that androgen produces a detailed plan or network in the brain that differs for males and females.

Gender Identity: The awareness of the distinctions between oneself and the opposite sex, and the perception of proper methods for interacting with the opposite sex.

Homosexuality: Sexual attraction to members of one's own sex.

Heterosexuality: Sexual attraction to members of the opposite sex.

Transsexuals: Individuals who wish to be rid of their genitals and secondary sex characteristics because they believe the opposite sex to be their true sex.

Male Hormones, Androgen and Testosterone: These tend to produce heightened levels of physical activity, sexual interest, and aggression.

Female Hormones, Estrogen and Progesterone: These influence physical changes related to the growth of long bones, ovulation, conception, menstruation, gestation, and vaginal lubrication.

Differential Sex Role Conditioning: Girls are taught to respond to verbal and non-verbal cues that it is permissible to cry and be comforted, to avoid rough and tumble activity, and to be passive and dependent while boys are taught to avoid feminine or "sissy" behavior, to suppress tears, and to gain approval through competition, aggressiveness, achievement, and independence.

Schoolbook Stereotypes of Masculinity and Femininity: Women are observers, shadowy figures, destined to be wives, mothers, or sisters. Boys are active adventurers, destined for interesting occupations.

Cultural Contradictions Affecting Sex Roles: Women are socialized to be passive, domestic, and subordinate despite frequent exposure to experience that leads them to recognize that women are as capable as men; men are socialized to be active and aggressive except in the area of emotion and tenderness which they are taught to inhibit rather than actively express.

LEARNING OBJECTIVES

Fill in the words required to complete each sentence.

Learning Objective 1

Describe basic genetic influences on gender differences and similarities.

a. There are between 120 and ____160____ conceptions of males per ____100____ females, a statistic that describes the __primary__ sex ratio.

b. The _Secondary_ sex ratio describes the _number_ of males per 100 females at the time of birth.

c. The proportion of males to females at adulthood is the _Tertiary_ sex ratio. At _older_ adult ages, women outnumber men.

d. Most recent research findings provide support for the belief that the greater _Logevity_ of women is partly _Biological_.

e. Males with XYY and _XXY_ chromosome structures are overrepresented in populations of maximum security _insitutions_. There is evidence from Denmark that men with such chromosomes may be of lower _intelligence_ and also more likely to commit crimes against _property_.

f. By the age of 12 ~~male~~ _weeks_, female infants tend to look longer at pictures of human _faces_ than at geometric patterns.

Learning Objective 2

Explain how different intrauterine processes influence gender development.

a. In the earliest _weeks_ of pregnancy, the embryo is not _differetiated_ as to sex.

b. Unless the fetal _testes_ secrete _androgen_ at a critical period, the fetus develops as a _female_.

c. _Progestians_ tend to have a _masculizing_ influence on female fetuses. Babies born with a mixture of male and female reproductive organs are called _hermophodites_.

d. The _androgenital_ syndrome results from a malfunction of the _adrenal_ glands.

e. Some long-term effects of fetal androgenization of females include _higher_ levels of I.Q., greater interest in _career_ than in marriage, and a _delayed_ interest in dating.

f. Scientists now believe that androgen may act on the _brain_, and that the _masculine_ brain may be programmed for assertiveness and higher _energy_ levels.

g. The seven-month-old male twin who penis was burned off was given a _female_ name and reared as a female with the aid of _estrogen_ therapy. In this case, _hormonal_ influences and _learning_ substantially overcame genetic influences.

Learning Objective 3

Describe the environmental contribution to the development of gender identity.

a. The development of masculine and feminine _personality_ characteristics is affected by complex _learning_ patterns that begin at _Birth_.

b. Parents intentionally and unintentionally _raise_ *or teach* young girls and boys different ways of acting, feeling, and _thinking_.

c. For example, many people admire signs of strength and _robustness_ in male babies, while _cutness_ is favored for female infants.

d. Today more parents make a _consious_ effort to treat boys and girls _alike_.

e. The term _gender_ identity refers to the person's definition of _self_ as either female or male. The _development_ of such identity is later crucial to the formation of _heterosexual_ relationships.

f. The child normally learns two sets of gender _roles_, one that he or she should _assume_ and the other which should be _responded_ to.

g. Successful _heterosexual_ relationships in adulthood are built on the foundation provided by _parental_ roles.

Learning Objective 4

Describe the most frequently occurring anomalies of gender identity.

a. There are many different kinds of homosexual _behavior_, requiring many different _explanation_. _Bisexuality_ is defined in terms of _comfortable_ sexual relationships with both women and men.

b. Some homosexual behavior, such as that among male _prisoners_, is seldom _repeated_ on the outside. Similarly, many _exclusivly_ heterosexual women may only participate in _homesexual_ activities during group-sex situations.

c. Additional causes of bisexuality seem to include the _Lesbian_ _XXY_ chromosome pattern in males, too much _androgen_ in females, and _ambigeus_ sex-role models who hinder the development of a clear _gender_ identity.

d. Transsexuals do not accept the gender of their _bodies_ and particularly reject their own _genetals_. The ratio of male to female transsexuals is at least _three_ to one, and it may be as high as _7 seven_ to one.

18

e. Since _Sexual_ development is more complex in _Male_ fetuses, it is also more easily _disturbed_.

f. Many transsexual men become _sexually_ active only if they adopt _homosexual_ behaviors.

g. The only successful _therapy_ for transsexuals is _sex-converse_ surgery, supplemented by _hormone_ treatments.

h. Converted transsexuals publicly assume the _role_ of their new _sex_ , and some eventually fall in love and _marry_ .

Learning Objective 5

Describe the experiences of early socialization that affect the development of gender identity.

a. Girls learn to respond to verbal and _nonverbal_ cues from _adults_ that bring _love_ and approval.

b. Young girls are less likely to behave ~~aggressively~~, and they develop ~~role~~ skills earlier than boys. Overall, adults ~~occupation~~ more ~~mothers~~ behavior in girls.

c. Boys are taught to give up their _identification_ with their mother, and that they must win approval through _achievement_. Boys are thus conditioned toward greater _aggression_ and _independence_.

d. As parents have become more _aware_ of sex differences in early _socialization_, many have attempted to _minimize_ these differences.

e. Many parents now view more _equality_ of the sexes as a benefit of eliminating sexist _child rearing_ practices.

f. _Traditionally_ masculine men will be less _occupationally_ focused, and husbands and wives may become more equal partners in earning a _living_ and maintaining a _home_.

Learning Objective 6

Describe the influence of public schools in the development of gender identity.

a. Schools generally reinforce and _extend_ the sex-role difference learned in the _home_. Boys are encouraged toward further aggression and _achievement_, girls toward more passivity and _domestically_

b. Schoolbooks tend to _Stereotype_ both masculine and feminine _Roles_.
Men, for example, are portrayed in active _occupational_ roles, while women are
presented chiefly as wives and _mothers_.

c. Teachers and counselors frequently give advice that prepares boys for
Careers and girls to be _Wives_.

d. Patricia Sexton views the schools as _Feminine_ institutions, and suggests
that most _Women_ school teachers overemphasize obedience and
Conformity in their pupils.

e. Sexton proposes that schools provide more _Men_ teachers as role
models for boys, and for increased liberation of _Women_.

f. Observation of children's play shows that boys are more likely than girls to
play _Outdoors_, in _Larger_ groups, in more mixed _Age_ groups,
in _Competitive_ games, and in _Longer_ games. In addition, _girls_
more often played in _boy's_ games, than vice versa.

g. The researchers concluded that boys' games aid preparation for _occupation_
success, while girls' games prepare participants for _Roles_ as wives
and mothers.

Learning Objective 7

Describe the cultural contradictions of traditional sex roles and more recent trends
toward role flexibility.

a. Adult _heterosexual_ relationships are built upon earlier sex-role _socialization_

b. Yet fulfilling adult relationships now confront men and women with _demands_
which are much less _traditional_.

c. Differences in masculine and feminine _personalities_ are socially created, but
recent social _trends_ are _reducing_ these differences.

d. By college age, many women still typically value love and _Approval_ more
than they value _Achievement_. They _fear_ that high achievement may
cause rejection, loss of _femininity_, and _emotional_ breakdown.

e. The tragedy of the emotionally _inexpressive_ male suggests that traditional views
of masculinity encourage men to fit one of two _stereotypes_, the cowboy or the
playboy.

f. However, the present trends are toward __Reduction__ of sex __diffnences__ in the future. One study, for example, has shown that men and women are giving more __Similian__ responses to the __Rorschach__ ink blot test. Adolescent boys and girls now associate more freely outside of the __formal__ dating situation, and it appears that young adults of both sexes are becoming more __Alike__. Finally, a recent study of college men has shown that the most preferred __confidents__ of intimate self-disclosure were their __women__ friends.

MULTIPLE CHOICE QUESTIONS

__A__ 1. The number of male conceptions for every 100 female conceptions is the _____ sex ratio.

    a. primary   c. tertiary
    b. secondary   d. XY

__C__ 2. The number of adult males for every 100 adult females is the _____ sex ratio.

    a. primary   c. tertiary
    b. secondary   d. XY

__b__ 3. Which of the following chromosome patterns does __not__ appear among males?

    a. the XY   c. the XXY
    b. the YY   d. the XYY

__D__ 4. Compared to XY men, XYY men were

    a. more likely to score higher in I.Q.
    b. less likely to commit violent crimes.
    c. more likely to commit violent crimes.
    d. more likely to commit crimes against property.

__A__ 5. The androgenital syndrome results from a deficiency of

    a. cortisol.   c. estrogen.
    b. androgen.   d. testosterone.

__C__ 6. Compared to normal girls, androgenital girls showed

    a. fewer career interests.
    b. higher interest in dating.
    c. higher I.Q. scores.
    d. few "tomboy" behaviors.

A 7. Which of the following was the last change for the male
        infant reared as a female?

        a. construction of an artificial vagina
        b. change to a girl's first name
        c. dressing in girl's clothes
        d. estrogen therapy

C
B 8. The environmental development of gender identity is probably most influenced
        by different _____ patterns.

        a. maturational   c. learning
        b. brain   d. eating

D 9. One's definition of self as either male or female is called a

        a. sex role.
        b. gender identity.
        c. sex-linked personality trait.
        d. sex-role stereotype.

C 10. Which of the following is not an anomaly of gender identity?

        a. homosexuality   c. transvestism
        b. bisexuality   d. transsexualism

A 11. With respect to sex differences in the numbers of transsexuals,

        a. men outnumber women.
        b. women outnumber men.
        c. women and men appear in approximately equal numbers.
        d. most older transsexuals are women, while younger transsexuals are men.

D 12. The most successful treatment for transsexuals is

        a. psychotherapy.
        b. heterosexual intercourse.
        c. homosexual intercourse.
        d. sex-conversion surgery.

B 13. Medical administration of testosterone most typically

        a. decreases the sex drive of both sexes.
        b. increases the sex drive of both sexes.
        c. increases the sex drive of men only.
        d. increases the sex drive of women only.

A 14. With respect to sex differences in the acquisition of language skills,

    a. girls develop more quickly than boys.
    b. boys develop more quickly than girls.
    c. both sexes develop at about the same time.
    d. boys respond to nonverbal language, while girls respond to verbal language.

C 15. As parents have become more aware of how sex differences develop, the most typical parental intention has been to

    a. encourage the development of further sex differences.
    b. do nothing and let nature take its course.
    c. minimize the development of existing sex differences.
    d. discourage sex play among younger children.

A 16. The idea that men should pursue careers, while women rear children, is an example of a

    a. stereotype.   c. sexual identity
    b. gender.   d. genetic anomaly.

A 17. Patricia Sexton believes that schools are basically _____ institutions.

    a. feminine   c. androgynous
    b. masculine   d. liberating

C 18. With respect to sex differences in children's play,

    a. girls are more likely to play outdoors.
    b. boys are more likely to play in smaller groups.
    c. boys are more likely to play longer games.
    d. girls are more likely to play in mixed-age groups.

D 19. Which of the following problems is the most likely outcome of traditional sex-role socialization?

    a. women who are emotionally inexpressive
    b. men who fear success
    c. men who "play dumb"
    d. men who are emotionally inexpressive

D 20. Which of the following statements is true?

    a. Women and men's responses to Rorschach ink blots are becoming more dissimilar.
    b. There is an increase in formal dating among adolescent boys and girls.

c. Masculine-feminine differences in personality have increased over the last decade.

d. College men increasingly prefer women as confidants for more intimate self-disclosure.

TRUE FALSE QUESTIONS

T 1. The number of males at birth per 100 females is the secondary sex ratio.

F 2. The greater life expectancy of women seems to result from the personality and social characteristics of each sex rather than innate biological differences.

F 3. Men with XYY and XXY chromosome patterns were more likely than normal men to commit violent crimes.

T 4. Male sexual development is more likely to include abnormalities.

F 5. Androgenital girls show lower average I.Q. scores than normal girls.

T 6. Gender identity is one's definition of self as either male or female.

T 7. The child normally learns two sets of gender roles.

F 8. Released male prisoners who have engaged in homosexual acts find it difficult to return to heterosexuality.

T 9. There are more male than female transsexuals.

F 10. The most successful treatment for transsexuals is psychotherapy.

F 11. Testosterone increases the sex drive of men and lowers the sex drive of women.

T 12. Boys are more likely than girls to play in mixed-age groups.

F 13. Many parents are trying to maximize the personality differences between their daughters and sons.

T 14. Much evidence suggests that American women and men are growing increasingly alike in personality.

MATCHING

_C_ 1. sex ratio   a. sense of oneself as male or female

_B_ 2. XXY and XYY chromosomes   b. lower I.Q.

_E_ 3. progestin   c. males per 100 females

_I_ 4. androgenital syndrome   d. male hormone

_A_ 5. gender identity   e. pregnancy-saving hormone

_D_ 6. androgen   f. female hormone

_F_ 7. progesterone   g. wanting to be the opposite sex

_h_ 8. inexpressive males   h. cowboy or playboy

_G_ 9. transsexualism   i. higher I.Q.

NAME MATCHING

_A_ 1. Patricia Cayo Sexton   a. studied public schools

_C_ 2. John Money   b. studied sex-role contradictions

_B_ 3. Mirra Komarovsky   c. studied androgenital girls

ESSAY QUESTIONS

1. Explain why the personality characteristics of men and women have become more alike. State which sex has changed most in the last two decades, and describe the recent social trends than have contributed to this change.

2. Explain why a firm sense of gender identity is crucial for individual development. Discuss the consequences for gender identity and subsequent heterosexual interaction if more parents continue to rear their sons and daughters alike.

3. Evaluate Patricia Cayo Sexton's thesis that schools feminize males. What are the individual and social consequences of such feminization?

ANSWERS

Learning Objective 1

a. 160, 100, primary
b. secondary, number
c. tertiary, older
d. longevity, biological
e. XXY, institutions, intelligence, property
f. weeks, faces

Learning Objective 2

a. weeks, differentiated
b. testes, androgen, female
c. progestins, masculinizing, hermaphrodites
d. androgenital, adrenal
e. higher, career, delayed
f. brain, masculine, energy
g. girl's, estrogen, hormonal, learning

Learning Objective 3

a. personality, learning, birth
b. teach, thinking
c. robustness, cuteness
d. conscious, alike
e. gender, self, development, heterosexual
f. roles, assume, responded
g. heterosexual, parental

Learning Objective 4

a. behavior, explanation, bisexuality, comfortable
b. prisoners, repeated, exclusively, lesbian
c. XXY, androgen, ambiguous, gender
d. bodies, genitals, three, seven
e. sexual, male, disturbed
f. sexually, homosexual
g. therapy, sex-conversion, hormone
h. role, sex, marry

Learning Objective 5

a. nonverbal, adults, love
b. aggressively, verbal, encourage, dependency
c. identification, achievement, aggression, independence

d. aware, socialization, minimize
e. equality, child-rearing
f. traditionally, occupationally, living, home

Learning Objective 6

a. extend, home, achievement, domesticity
b. stereotype, roles, occupational, mothers
c. careers, wives
d. feminine, women, conformity
e. men, models, women
f. outdoors, larger, age, competitive, longer, girls, boys'

g. occupational, roles

Learning Objective 7

a. heterosexual, socialization
b. demands, traditional
c. personalities, trends, reducing
d. approval, achievement, fear, femininity, emotional
e. inexpressive, stereotypes, playboy
f. reduction, differences, similar, Rorschach, formal, alike, confidants, women

MULTIPLE CHOICE QUESTIONS

1.	a	11.	a
2.	c	12.	d
3.	b	13.	b
4.	d	14.	a
5.	a	15.	c
6.	c	16.	a
7.	a	17.	a
8.	c	18.	c
9.	b	19.	d
10.	c	20.	d

TRUE FALSE QUESTIONS

1.	T	8.	F
2.	F	9.	T
3.	F	10.	F
4.	T	11.	F
5.	F	12.	T
6.	T	13.	F
7.	T	14.	T

MATCHING

1.	c	6.	d
2.	b	7.	f
3.	e	8.	h
4.	i	9.	g
5.	a		

NAME MATCHING

1.	a
2.	c
3.	b

Chapter 3

PAIRING OFF

KEY TERMS AND CONCEPTS

Masculine Subculture: The male peer group in which sexual activity is discussed in personal terms and is encouraged through sharing accounts of sexual exploits.

Competition for Status: Boys gain status by sexual activity; girls gain status by attractiveness to boys and restraint in behavior.

Early Dating: Pre-teenage dating is reminiscent of teenage dating patterns of the 1950s and 1960s. Youngsters idealize one person as a future marital partner.

High School Dating: The high school patterns include those who don't date, those "playing the field," and those who are "going steady." Groups have gatherings where the lack of explicit pairing off allows unpaired members to participate.

High School Marriages: These marriages largely occur among those who are not destined for college. A high proportion of these teenage marriages follow premarital pregnancy.

Traditional Dating: Dating patterns which involve sexual bargaining and which are modeled after parents and other adults.

Values in Dating: The positive experiences of youngsters who date different persons in the process of learning to evaluate traits that will make good marriage partners.

Even Bargains: Most dating is equal in that the most attractive, high-socioeconomic status women have dates with the most attractive, high-status men.

Principle of Least Interest: The partner who is least interested in continuing the dating relationship has a measure of control over the other.

The Function of Lovers' Quarrels: The partner in an unequal relationship will become aware of exploitation. Such awareness sets the stage for a quarrel which either terminates dating or reduces the exploitation.

Companionship Dating: A relationship in the 1960s and 1970s in which the woman acted as a sympathetic listener, participated in some sexual activities, and joined in the search for identity within the context of private rather than public activities.

Instrumental Dating: A relationship in the 1960s in which males sought opportunities for sexual conquest. In the 1970s, male interest in women switched to a desire for political activity, drug use, and lovemaking.

Traditional Dating: A relationship in the 1960s and 1970s in which the man was consciously looking for qualities suitable in a wife.

Intellectual Dating: A relationship of the 1960s and 1970s which emphasized the woman's intellectual capabilities and her ability to share ideas.

Interfaith Dating: Dating between members of two different religions and which is supported by most young people.

Interracial Dating: Dating between members of different races, a practice gaining increasing acceptance. Three times as many blacks approve as do whites, but white approval has risen dramatically in recent years.

College Marriages: Marriages which occur while one or both partners are still in college. These marriages are vulnerable to such problems as unexpected pregnancies, growing divergence of interest, and lower marital satisfaction for the student wife.

LEARNING OBJECTIVES

Fill in the words required to complete each sentence.

Learning Objective 1

Describe the characteristics of pre-teen relationships between boys and girls.

a. Children develop an __Interest__ in persons of the __opposite__ sex at an early age. The __personality__ foundations for heterosexual __interaction__ are established early, and some children experience romantic __attraction__ before they start __school__ .

b. Boys are more likely than girls to share their __sexual__ experiences with their __peers__ . However, a girl's success in __attracting__ boys secures her approval and __status__ from others.

c. Boys require little _ecurAgment_ to become interested in _sex_ . For
example, boys are more likely to handle their _genital_ and to discuss their
sexual desires with their _peers_ .

d. There is some _hostility_ toward females in these discussions, and women are
frequently portrayed as sexually _wanton_ or deliberately _frustrating_ .

e. _sexual_ accomplishment brings _status_ in boys' groups. Yet considerable _anxiety_ is also generated by sexual exaggeration, and group
pressures lead to a sexual orientation that is exploitative and _self centered_

f. Girls do not usually gain _status_ through sexual _activity_ . The
sexually active girl often cannot _compete_ successfully in other ways, and
the _attitude_ of her female peers may be _disapproving_

g. Girls seek approval from _Approval_ and use that approval to create
envy in other girls!

h. Girls learn that attractiveness to _Boys_ and sexual _Restrain_ brings
the most approval from _Adults_ and peers.

Learning Objective 2

Describe the basic findings of studies on early dating.

a. Many 10-to-12-year-olds _Intimate_ older _Dating_ patterns.

b. Many fifth- and sixth-grade children are already _emotionally_ involved with
the _opposite_ sex. Often they have already _selected_ one person, whom
they view in the context of future _marriage_ . The _Majority_ of these
students also report having been in _love_ .

c. _Urban_ youngsters from higher _economic_ groups begin dating earliest,
but most _dating_ activities at this age are rather _structured_.

d. A recent study of high schools showed that about one student in _10_
does not _date_ . The two largest dating categories were "playing the
feld " and "going _steady_ ." Over _2/3_ of the students
dated only occasionally.

e. Many young people are increasingly _critical_ of the _traditional_ dating
system. They seek instead to know one another better as _people_ .

f. _Pair_ dating is being partly replaced by _group_ gatherings of
young people. These permit individuals to be _included_ without worry about
being _Accepted_

g. Boys and girls are also discouraged from "playing little __games__," though some __couples__ may withdraw to have more __private__ time together.

Learning Objective 3

Describe the basic characteristics of high-school marriages.

a. Few __young__ marriages occur among people destined to become __college__ students. These students are __advised__ to complete their __education__ and start their __careers__ before any serious emotional involvement.

b. Noncollege students frequently share intimate __sexual__ involvements and __marry__ early.

c. Only about __8,000__ young men under age 18 marry in the United States each __year__, but about __130,000__ young women marry under the age of 18.

d. In __42%__ percent of the marriages of 15-to-19-year-old __brides__, a child is born in less than __8__ months. __Infant__ mortality __rates__ are also higher for these very young mothers.

e. Arrival of a child frequently confirms the young __husbands__ plan to work without seeking further __education__.

f. Early marriage, lack of __formal__ education, and __early__ childbearing combine to keep the family at __inadequte__ income levels. Compared to older marriages, __teenage__ marriages are about __twice__ as likely to end in divorce.

Learning Objective 4

Describe patterns of dating among college students.

a. Many youths are __advised__ that positive __values__ may be obtained from college __dating__ experience.

b. Young people who date are advised to de-emphasize __sex__, good __look__, and possession of __money__. Instead, they are urged to evaluate __dates__ for traits that suggest a good __marriage__ partner.

c. The characteristic of women ranked as most important by __college__ men is dependable __canater__. College women rank emotional __stability__ as the most important characteristic of their future husbands. The rankings of women and men were remarkably __close__.
__similare__

d. In __traditional__ dating interactions, men most often bargain for __sex__,
and women bargain to __marry__ as well as possible. Men and women generally
strike fairly __even__ bargains by dating at their own levels of
__ATTRACTIVNESS__

e. The __principle__ of least __interest__ dictates which partner has more power.
the partner with more ~~least~~ __(most interest)__ involvement has ~~more~~ __less__ power.

f. The purpose of lovers' quarrels is to __terminate__ the relationship or to
minimize __exploytation__

g. Lovers' quarrels are most likely to occur when the __power__ in a relationship is greatly out of __balance__ .

Learning Objective 5

Describe the newly emerging norms that govern college dating.

a. Data from college classes of 1964 and 1965 reveal four distinct dating
__patterns__: companionship, instrumental, __traditional__ and __intellectual__.

b. The companionship pattern emphasized private and __intimate__ activities.
__Sexual__ activity appeared to be subordinate to the couple's search for
__Identity__.

c. In the instrumental dating pattern, the masculine __subculture__ was dominant,
and the men were primarily interested in __Sexual__ conquest.

d. In the traditional pattern, men dated women who were of equal __Status__
and religiously and sexually __CONSERVATIVE__

e. The intellectual pattern was found among __brilliant__ but socially
__Inexperienced__ men.

f. More recent data have shown that the __Intellectual__ and __Companionship__ dating
patterns have remained unchanged.

g. The instrumental pattern has changed to emphasize __political__ activism and
__drug__ use in addition to sexual activity.

h. While more men now date, they often resist __Commitment__ to a particular woman
because of needs for several additional years of __professional__ preparation.
However, their girlfriends feel that their __College__ years offered the
best opportunities for making good __marriages__.

Learning Objective 6

Describe interreligious and interracial dating among young adults.

a. Twenty-five years ago, about _half_ of all young people were willing to marry outside of their _religion_. By 1971, _91_ percent said they would do so.

b. Growing numbers of today's young adults view interfaith dating as an _opportunity_ rather than a _problem_.

c. Much interfaith dating among _College_ students is not under _parental_ supervision.

d. By 1971, about one person in _five_ had dated _interacially_. Greatest acceptance of dating between races is found among the _young_, more affluent, and the better _educated_.

e. About _20_ percent of whites and _60_ percent of blacks approve of interracial _marriage. or dating_

f. In a high school study of interracial dating, it was found that _Black_ girls seldom dated _white_ boys.

g. School authorities did not interfere with interracial dating among lower _status_ students, but they were often _coercive_ toward upper _status_ students.

Learning Objective 7

Describe the basic findings from studies of college marriages.

a. About _20_ percent of today's college students are married. College marriages occur most often in _urban_ universities and among _upperclassmen_

b. One study suggests that about _30_ percent of all college marriages follow premarital _pregnancy_. Completion of _education_ and _marital_ adjustment is often complicated by early childbearing.

c. From 1945 to 1955 the typical college marriage involved a war _veteran_ who studied under the _GI_ Bill.

d. The next pattern of college marriage involved completion of the husband's _education_, while the wife took a _job_.

e. By the _1970's_, a more _egalitarian_ form of college marriage emerged: both husband and wife _worked_ and continued their studies.

34

f. There was more evidence of ~~commitment~~ _Strain_ in the marriages in which the ~~wives professed~~ continued their ___education___. However, this finding tells us nothing about the ___quality___ of egalitarian marriages over a longer ___time___ span.

MULTIPLE CHOICE QUESTIONS

_C_ 1. Compared to girls, boys are generally more likely to share their hetero-
         sexual experiences with their

         a. mothers.   c. peers.
         b. fathers.   d. school teachers.

_b_ 2. The groups in which boys share their sexual fantasies are a part of the
         masculine

         a. mystique.   c. society.
         b. subculture.   d. personality.

_A_ 3. Girls ordinarily win status from adults and other girls through attractive-
         ness to boys and sexual

         a. restraint.   c. frustration.
         b. teasing.   d. experience.

_A_ 4. A recent study has shown that about _____ percent of high school
         students do not date.

         a. 11   c. 31
         b. 21   d. 41

_C_ 5. Which of the following is most characteristic of high school marriages?

         a. delayed childbearing   c. higher divorce rates
         b. higher income level   d. continued formal education

_D_ 6. About _____ percent of all boys and girls have their first date
         between the ages of 13 and 15.

         a. 5   c. 35
         b. 20   d. 50

_d_ 7. Which of the following was ranked as <u>least</u> important by college students who described the characteristics they sought in their future spouses?

    a. dependable character   c. good health
    b. refinement   d. chastity

_A_ 8. In the traditional dating situation, men bargain for _____ and women bargain for _____ .

    a. sex, marriage.
    b. good looks, money.
    c. status, intimacy.
    d. freedom, control.

_D_ 9. The principle of least _____ dictates the balance of _____ in a dating relationship.

    a. intimacy, attractiveness
    b. attractiveness, intimacy
    c. power, interest
    d. interest, power

_C_ 10. Dating between partners from different status levels frequently leads to increased

    a. competition.   c. exploitation.
    b. cooperation.   d. gratification.

_A_ 11. A procedure for terminating dating relationships or minimizing future exploitation is

    a. the lovers' quarrel.   c. playing the field.
    b. premarital intercourse.   d. going steady.

_D_ 12. A lovers' quarrel most frequently occurs when a relationship is out of balance with respect to

    a. affection.   c. commitment.
    b. sexual gratification.   d. power.

_C_ 13. Which of the following is <u>not</u> a distinct dating pattern of Harvard men?

    a. companionship   c. emotional
    b. traditional   d. intellectual

A 14. Which of the following pairs of dating patterns changed most from the 1960s to the 1970s?

 a. the traditional and instrumental
 b. the companionship and intellectual
 c. the intellectual and instrumental
 d. the traditional and companionship

B 15. About 91 percent of young adults are willing to marry a partner of a different

 a. race.   c. social class.
 b. religion.   d. political party.

C 16. Which of the following is most characteristic of people who accept interracial dating?

 a. lower income   c. higher education
 b. higher age   d. rural residence

C 17. About _____ as many blacks as whites approve of interracial marriage.

 a. one-half   c. three times
 b. twice   d. four times

C 18. School authorities are most accepting of interracial dating between students who are

 a. good athletes.   c. lower status.
 b. college oriented.   d. higher status.

d 19. The egalitarian college marriage was most common in the

 a. 1940s.   c. 1960s.
 b. 1950s.   d. 1970s.

B 20. Compared to women who drop out of school, college wives who continue their education report

 a. higher marital satisfaction.
 b. lower marital satisfaction.
 c. fewer problems with children.
 d. fewer employment problems.

TRUE FALSE QUESTIONS

F 1. Boys require more encouragement than girls to become interested in sex.

T 2. Boys frequently gain status with their peers through sexual exaggeration and sexual activity.

F 3. Group dating is being replaced to some extent by pair dating.

T 4. Men and women appear to be seeking very similar qualities in their future spouses.

F 5. College men rate chastity as the most important characteristic of their future wives.

T 6. The principle of least interest determines the balance of power in a dating relationship.

F 7. Dating relationships between partners of equal status are most likely to become exploitative.

F 8. A recent study of Harvard men has found six distinct dating patterns.

T 9. Interreligious dating is generally more acceptable than interracial dating.

F 10. The most frequent type of interracial dating is between black girls and white boys.

F 11. More college marriages than high school marriages are preceded by pregnancy.

T 12. The egalitarian college marriage was most common in the 1970s.

F 13. Compared to dropouts, college wives who continue their studies report higher marital satisfaction.

MATCHING

_e_ 1. masculine subculture   a. change from pair to group dating

_A_ 2. new dating norms   b. approved by 91 percent of students

_g_ 3. teenage marriage   c. balance of power

_J_ 4. dating values   d. ends exploitation

_C_ 5. principle of least interest   e. boys' peer groups

_D_ 6. lovers' quarrels   f. tolerated for lower status students

_I_ 7. changing dating patterns   g. 42 percent preceded by pregnancy

_B_ 8. interfaith marriage   h. more egalitarian

_F_ 9. interracial dating   i. traditional and instrumental

_H_ 10. college marriage   j. quite similar for men and women

ESSAY QUESTIONS

1. While the traditional dating system encourages competition, marriage seeking, and sexual exploitation, more recent dating norms have emphasized sexual, intellectual, and emotional sharing, and a cooperative search for personal and pair identity. Describe the social conditions that provide support for each type of dating pattern.

2. How well do the principles of bargaining, least interest, balance of power, and exploitation describe the second dating pattern described in the previous question?

3. Explain why interfaith marriage has now won nearly universal acceptance among young adults.

ANSWERS

Learning Objective 1

a. interest, opposite, personality, interaction, attraction, school

b. sexual, peers, attracting, status
c. encouragement, sex, genitals, peers
d. hostility, wanton, frustrating
e. sexual, status, anxiety, self-centered
f. status, activity, compete, attitude, disapproving
g. adults, envy
h. boys, restraint, adults

Learning Objective 2

a. imitate, dating
b. emotionally, opposite, selected, marriage, majority, love

c. urban, socioeconomic, dating, structured
d. 10, date, field, steady, one-third
e. critical, traditional, people
f. pair, group, included, accepted
g. games, couples, private

Learning Objective 3

a. young, college, advised, education, careers
b. sexual, marry
c. 18,000, year, 130,000
d. 42, brides, eight, infant, rates
e. husband's, education
f. formal, early, inadequate, teenage, twice

Learning Objective 4

a. advised, values, dating
b. sex, looks, money, dates, marriage
c. college, character, stability, similar
d. traditional, sex, marry even, attractiveness
e. principle, interest, emotional, less
f. terminate, exploitation
g. power, balance

Learning Objective 5

a. patterns, traditional, intellectual
b. intimate, sexual, identity
c. subculture, sexual
d. status, conservative
e. brilliant, inexperienced
f. intellectual, companionship
g. political, drug
h. commitment, professional, college, marriages

Learning Objective 6

a. half, religion, 91
b. opportunity, problem
c. college, parental
d. five, interracially, young, educated
e. 20, 60, marriage
f. black, white
g. status, coercive, status

Learning Objective 7

a. 20, urban, upperclassmen
b. 30, pregnancy, education, marital
c. veteran, G.I.
d. education, job
e. 1970s, egalitarian, worked
f. strain, wives, education, quality, time

MULTIPLE CHOICE QUESTIONS

1.	c	11.	a
2.	b	12.	d
3.	a	13.	c
4.	a	14.	a
5.	c	15.	b
6.	d	16.	c
7.	d	17.	c
8.	a	18.	c
9.	d	19.	d
10.	c	20.	b

TRUE FALSE QUESTIONS

1.	F	8.	F
2.	T	9.	T
3.	F	10.	F
4.	T	11.	F
5.	F	12.	T
6.	T	13.	F
7.	F		

MATCHING

1.	e	6.	d
2.	a	7.	i
3.	g	8.	b
4.	j	9.	f
5.	c	10.	h

Chapter 4

SEXUAL INVOLVEMENT

KEY TERMS AND CONCEPTS

<u>Infant Sexual Behavior</u>: Sexual responses that occur in infants such as penile erections and vaginal lubrication.

<u>Preadolescent Sexual Behavior</u>: Sexual activity, most commonly masturbation, during the childhood years.

<u>Sexual Conditioning</u>: Influences which lead boys toward a focus on genital pleasure and girls toward a focus on relationships and romance.

<u>Masturbation</u>: Manipulation of the genitals which may be continued until orgasm is achieved.

<u>Pornography</u>: Books, pictures, films, or any other kind of material that presents explicit sex in a manner that can be described as obscene or morally offensive.

<u>Venereal Disease</u>: Diseases transmitted through contact with the genitals, the most common being syphilis, gonorrhea, and Herpes II.

<u>Syphilis</u>: An infectious venereal disease which, if left untreated, passes through three stages. The first is characterized by a hard chancre (sore) at the point of entrance of the microorganism (called spirochete); the second by lesions of the skin and mucous membranes; and the third by the disablement and infection of bones, muscles, and nerve tissue.

<u>Gonorrhea</u>: A venereal disease characterized by inflammation of the mucous membrane of the genito-urinary tract and a discharge of mucus and pus. It can seriously affect other mucous membranes such as a baby's eyes during childbirth.

<u>Herpes II</u>: A disease that produces painful genital blisters and recurring virus attacks. Presently there is no effective cure.

<u>Coed Dorm Living</u>: Dorm living in which students of both sexes live in the same housing in a casual, relaxed environment which helps to avoid the artificiality of traditional dating.

<u>Living Together</u>: Behaviors of an unmarried couple ranging from casual sex to entry into structured, lasting relationships.

LEARNING OBJECTIVES

Fill in the words required to complete each sentence.

Learning Objective 1

Describe recent research findings on childhood sexual behavior.

a. In the 1950s, Alfred <u>Kinsey</u> and his associates reported orgasm-like responses in <u>INFANTS</u> who were about four <u>Mouths</u> old.

b. More recent studies have shown frequent penile <u>erections</u> among <u>INFANT</u> boys and vaginal <u>LubRicATIoN</u> among girls.

c. Other researchers estimate that about 75 percent of the population have engaged in <u>Childhood</u> sex <u>PlAY</u>.

d. Differences between boys and girls in <u>Sexuality</u> appear to have been <u>Overestimated</u>

e. The masculine <u>Subculture</u> encourages boys to define sex in terms of <u>geNetAl</u> pleasure, while girls are taught to view sex in the context of <u>RomaNtic</u> relationships.

f. Simon and Gagnon report that males often seek sex in <u>CASUAl</u> relationships, while females accept it in more <u>STAble</u> ones. For example, males typically reported <u>INtercours</u> one to three times with their first sexual <u>PARTNer</u>, while women reported <u>teN</u> or more times with their first partners.

Learning Objective 2

Describe recent findings on adolescent sexual behavior.

a. About <u>89</u> percent of males and <u>61</u> percent of females reported presently engaging in <u>INtercourse</u>

b. About <u>20</u> percent of both sexes report continued masturbation in addition to regular sexual <u>ActiviTY</u> with a <u>PARTNer</u>.

c. The majority of those who masturbate report _Pleasure_ satisfaction, but a large minority of respondents reported feeling guilt or _depression_

d. About _75_ percent of all young people see _pornographic_ materials by the age of 18. When viewing such materials, females report as _much_ and as _frequent_ arousal as males.

e. People exposed to pornography show no more sexual _activity_ following exposure than _before_ exposure. Compared to normals, adult sex _offenders_ reported _lower_ exposure to _pornography_ during adolescence.

f. Overexposure to pornography leads to _Boredom_, and the commission urged _Repeal_ of all laws limiting _Adult_ access to pornography.

g. Attitudes toward _premarital_ sexual _intercourse_ have grown more approving in recent years, and college students have become much more accepting of such sexual activities as heavy _petting_, intercourse, and _oral genital_ contacts.

Learning Objective 3

Describe the conditions that determine extent of participation in sexual intercourse.

a. In the Michigan studies of 1969 and 1973, about _1/3_ of the boys and girls had engaged in sexual intercourse. _Rates_ of intercourse increased for _females_, but decreased for _males_ during the study.

b. The overall _gap_ in sexual experience between college women and men is _narrowing_.

c. Over _one half_ of all men report first intercourse with a partner whom they did not _love_, but _4/5_ of women report loving their first partner. Almost _1/2_ of the women planned to _marry_ their first partner.

d. In a recent model developed to explain premarital sex among college students, the five most important causes were _Religious_ values, fraternity/sorority _affiliation_, off-camput residence, dating _frequency_, and emotional _commitment_ to a partner.

e. The most likely _site_ of first intercourse is the woman's _residence_. Women are more likely to report _anxiety_ during their first experience, and only about _3/5_ of the women were happy with their first experience.

f. More women than men reported that intercourse _strengthened_ their _relationship_ with their partners.

g. _Contraceptive_ protection was inadequate for about _2/3_ of first sexual experiences, and _men_ were about three times more likely to use birth control.

Learning Objective 4

Describe the emotional dynamics of early sexual experience.

a. In the traditional dating pattern, men pursue women for _physical_ pleasure and feelings of _conquest_, and women are concerned about _exploitation_. Men were more likely than women to tell several _friends_ about their first _intercourse_.

b. Young people increasingly use sex to _find_ one another, but they try to view it as just one part of the _total_ experience of others.

c. Adolescence is an important time for receiving confirmation from one's _peers_ that one is _adequate_ and desirable. Men frequently seek this confirmation through _sexual_ activity, but the _self esteem_ of women still depends on greater restraint.

d. Some recent changes have partially freed men from the need for sexual _conquest_ and women are more likely to respond from their true _feelings_.

e. Yet as relationships become more _equalitarian_ the _self esteem_ of both men and women is increasingly linked to _capable_ sexual performance.

f. Confirmed _virginity_ has increasingly come to suggest such problems as personal immaturity and _homosexuality_ tendencies. But it appears that some young people seek to overcome their own _anxieties_ by _coercing_ others into premarital sex.

g. There is no evidence that premarital sex is related to subsequent _personal_ and _marital_ adjustment. Compared to casual sex, _loving_ sex is more independent of _performance_ standards.

Learning Objective 5

Describe several important complications of premarital sex.

a. _Venereal_ disease has become almost _epidemic_, _illegitimate_ births are more common, and more pregnancies are being _aborted_.

b. The two most common forms of venereal disease are _siphilis_ and _gonorea_.

c. _Herpes_ II is an especially problematic disease because there is presently no effective prevention or _Cure_ for it.

d. The most serious complication of Herpes II is an increased _Probability_ of _Cervical_ cancer.

e. About _2/3_ of the population has approved of providing contraception to _sexually_ active _unmarried_ teenagers. The most widely used method of contraception by unmarried _teenage_ women is the _pill_.

f. Of women reporting _premarital_ coitus before the age of 20, about _30_ percent became pregnant. Of these women who did not _marry_, about _60_ percent had live births, and _20_ percent had abortions.

Learning Objective 6

Describe the basic patterns of heterosexual interaction in coed dormitory living.

a. By _1974_, it was estimated that more than _½_ of the nation's resident college students lived in coed dorms.

b. In coed dorms, there appears to be more _group_ interaction and less _____ interaction.

c. Many women like being treated by their male dormmates as human beings rather than sexual _conquests_; other women miss the _pursuit_ aspect of more _traditional_ dating.

d. Frequently those who have _sex_ choose their partners from outside the _intimate_ dorm _group_. Most sex within coed dorms appears to be _monogomos_, and it involves _emotional_ intimacy and deep _comitment_.

e. Believing that sexual involvement implies _emotional_ involvement, many dormmates of both sexes are not attracted to _casual_ sex.

Learning Objective 7

Describe the characteristics of couples who live together.

a. Data from the _Cencus_ indicate that about _1,000,000_ couples are presently living together.

b. About _1/4_ of all _college_ students have lived with someone, and cohabitation appears to be far more common among students than in the general _population_.

c. Many couples deny that cohabitation indicates future __MARRIAGE__ , and no __PERMANENT__ commitment is often the norm.

d. The most common arrangement is for the __WOMAN__ to partially move in with the __MAN__ . This hides the arrangement from __PARENTS__ . Few couples share __FINANCES__ completely, and __UNEQUAL__ division of domestic labor is often a source of disagreement.

e. Most partners state that cohabitation has provided __EMOTIONAL__ growth, and that they would not consider __MARRIAGE__ before living together first.

f. The sexual problems of cohabitating couples are quite __SIMILAR__ to the problems of __MARRIED__ couples.

g. The experience of __COMMUNAL__ living is not usually very __RADICAL__ nor does it last long.

h. One way to avoid true __INTIMACY__ is to espouse a philosophy of __SEXUAL__ freedom and to engage in sex __INDISCRIMATILY__

MULTIPLE CHOICE QUESTIONS

__C__ 1. The first cases of sexual activity in human infants were reported by

    a. William Masters.   c. Alfred Kinsey.
    b. Virginia Johnson.   d. Chad Gordon.

__D__ 2. In the 1960s it was demonstrated that female infants frequently experience vaginal

    a. resolution.   c. excitation.
    b. inflammation.   d. lubrication.

__C__ 3. Simon and Gagnon estimate that about _____ percent of all persons engage in childhood sex play.

    a. 45   c. 75
    b. 60   d. 90

__A__ 4. More than half of all students of both sexes report engaging in _____ by the age of 13.

    a. masturbation   c. sex fantasy
    b. intercourse   d. petting

___C__ 5. Individuals classified as _____ are less likely to have seen pornography than the general population.

    a. sexually active   c. sex offenders
    b. politically liberal   d. less religious

___B__ 6. According to attitude surveys, which of the following sexual activities has __not__ received increasing approval from southern and midwestern college students?

    a. heavy petting   c. sexual intercourse
    b. sadomasochism   d. oral-genital sex

___B__ 7. The difference in sexual experiences of college women and men appears to be

    a. widening.   c. remaining constant.
    b. narrowing.   d. widening for intercourse, but narrowing for other sexual behaviors.

___C__ 8. Which of the following variables does __not__ enter the causal model for explaining premarital intercourse among college students?

    a. religious values
    b. fraternity/sorority affiliation
    c. intensity of sex drive
    d. off-campus residence

___A__ 9. First sexual intercourse is most likely to occur

    a. at the woman's residence.
    b. at the man's residence.
    c. in an automobile.
    d. in a motel.

___A__ 10. Following first intercourse, about two-thirds of the women felt their relationship had

    a. been strengthened.   c. remained unchanged.
    b. been weakened.   d. been terminated.

___D__ 11. About ____90____ percent of all women report planning no contraception for their first intercourse.

    a. 30   c. 70
    b. 50   d. 90

C 12. Premarital intercourse appears to be _____ to subsequent personal and marital adjustment.

    a. positively related   c. completely unrelated
    b. negatively related   d. indirectly related

B 13. Which reason was most often stated by women as their reason for abstaining from premarital intercourse?

    a. fear of pregnancy   c. moral beliefs
    b. absence of love   d. feelings of shame

A 14. Which reason was most often stated by men as their reason for abstaining from premarital intercourse?

    a. fear of pregnancy   c. moral beliefs
    b. absence of love   d. feelings of shame

C 15. Which of the following is not a venereal disease?

    a. syphilis   c. Herpes I
    b. gonorrhea   d. Herpes II

A 16. The most serious complication of Herpes II is an increased probability of

    a. cervical cancer.   c. nongonoccoccal urethritis.
    b. breast cancer.   d. yeast infection.

D 17. The contraceptive technique used most frequently by sexually active unmarried women is the

    a. diaphragm.   c. IUD.
    b. condom.   d. pill.

B 18. With respect to coed dormitory living,

    a. there is more pair dating than group dating.
    b. some women appear to miss traditional dating.
    c. the practice has been in decline since 1974.
    d. most couples are sexually promiscuous.

D 19. Which of the following is most characteristic of living together?

    a. The couples share finances completely.
    b. The man usually moves into the woman's residence.
    c. Virtually all couples plan to marry.
    d. Sexual problems are quite similar to those of married couples.

50

TRUE FALSE QUESTIONS

_F_ 1. Most recent research indicates larger differences in the sexuality of boys and girls than were previously assumed.

_F_ 2. A majority of students who masturbate report feelings of guilt or depression.

_F_ 3. Compared to normal adults, convicted sex offenders were more likely to have been exposed to pornography during adolescence.

_T_ 4. Public attitudes toward premarital sex have become more approving in recent years.

_T_ 5. The majority of women report being in love with their first sex partners.

_F_ 6. The majority of men planned to marry their first sex partners.

_T_ 7. Fear of pregnancy is the reason most often given by men for abstaining from premarital intercourse.

_T_ 8. The most serious complication of Herpes II is an increased probability of cervical cancer.

_T_ 9. The pill is the contraceptive most often used by unmarried teenage women.

_F_ 10. About one-half of all women use contraception during their first sexual intercourse.

_T_ 11. The sexual problems of couples who live together are quite similar to sexual problems reported by married couples.

MATCHING

_C_ 1. infant sexuality   a. 50 percent by age 19

_e_ 2. pornography   b. spirochete infection

_G_ 3. masturbation   c. penile erection and vaginal lubrication

_A_ 4. premarital intercourse   d. one million couples

_i_ 5. gonorrhea   e. used less often by sex offenders

_b_ 6. syphilis   f. genital blisters

_f_ 7.   Herpes II

_D_ 8.   coed dormitories

_h_ 9.   living together

g.   50 percent by age 13

h.   monogamous sexuality

i.   inflammation of the urinary-genital
    tract

NAME MATCHING

_A_ 1.   Alfred Kinsey

_C_ 2.   William Masters and Virginia
      Johnson

_B_ 3.   William Simon and John Gagnon

a.   studied infant sexual responses

b.   studied first intercourse

c.   reported infant vaginal lubrication

ESSAY QUESTIONS

1.   Describe the differences in training that lead boys and girls to different
attitudes toward sexuality, and discuss the future of these differences if
recent trends toward nonsexist childrearing practices are continued.

2.   Discuss the impact of pornography on sex offenses and other types of anti-social
behavior.

3.   Describe the individual consequences of first sexual intercourse for men and
women. To what extent are these consequences related to the differences in
training indicated in the first essay question?

ANSWERS

Learning Objective 1

a. Kinsey, infants, months
b. erections, infant, lubrication
c. childhood, play
d. sexuality, overestimated
e. subculture, genital, romantic
f. casual, stable, intercourse, partner, ten

Learning Objective 2

a. 89, 61, masturbation
b. 20, activity, partner
c. physical, depression
d. 75, pornographic, much, frequent
e. activity, before, offenders, lower, pornography
f. boredom, repeal, adult
g. premarital, intercourse, petting, oral-genital

Learning Objective 3

a. one-third, rates, females, males
b. gap, narrowing
c. one-half, love, four-fifths, one-half, marry
d. religious, affiliation, frequency, commitment
e. site, residence, anxiety, three-fifths
f. strengthened, relationship
g. contraceptive, two-thirds, men

Learning Objective 4

a. physical, conquest, exploitation, friends, intercourse
b. find, total
c. peers, adequate, sexual, self-esteem
d. conquest, feelings
e. equalitarian, self-esteem, capable
f. virginity, homosexuality, anxieties, coercing
g. personal, marital, loving, performance

Learning Objective 5

a. venereal, epidemic, illegitimate, aborted
b. syphilis, gonorrhea
c. herpes, cure
d. probability, cervical
e. two-thirds, sexually, unmarried, teenage, pill
f. premarital, 30, marry, 60, 20

Learning Objective 6

a. 1974, one-half
b. group, interactions
c. conquests, pursuit, traditional
d. sex, intimate, group, monogamous, emotional, commitment
e. emotional, casual

Learning Objective 7

a. census, 1,000,000
b. one-fourth, college, population
c. marriage, permanent
d. woman, man, parents, finances, unequal
e. emotional, marriage
f. similar, married
g. communal, radical
h. intimacy, sexual, indiscriminately

MULTIPLE CHOICE QUESTIONS

1.	c	10.	a
2.	d	11.	d
3.	c	12.	c
4.	a	13.	b
5.	c	14.	a
6.	b	15.	c
7.	b	16.	a
8.	c	17.	d
9.	a	18.	b
		19.	d

TRUE FALSE QUESTIONS

1.	F	7.	T
2.	F	8.	T
3.	F	9.	T
4.	T	10.	F
5.	T	11.	T
6.	F		

MATCHING

1.	c	6.	b
2.	e	7.	f
3.	g	8.	h
4.	a	9.	d
5.	i		

NAME MATCHING

1. a
2. c
3. b

Chapter 5

LOVE: THE SEARCH FOR FULFILLMENT

KEY TERMS AND CONCEPTS

Love: Describes various positive feelings of emotion which may take such forms as helpless dependence, cooperative support, or passionate interaction.

Developmental Tasks: Describes periods in the life of an individual during which specific social and emotional skills are acquired before moving on to the next stage.

Infant Stage: The dependent infant responds with pleasure to the nurturing care associated with the physical comfort of being fed, washed, clothed, held, and cuddled.

Early Childhood Stage: The growing child forms a view of self as female or male and as a person able to give as well as receive love.

Oedipal Stage: A period during which children are attracted to parents of the opposite sex. This period provides a rehearsal for eroticism in future relationships.

Preadolescent Stage: A period when same-sex friends become confidants about yearnings toward members of the opposite sex.

Youth Stage: Overt identification with same-sex adult role models who are often idealized. Idealization is often transferred to heterosexual relationships.

Teenage and Young Adult Stage: Idealization of specific members of the opposite sex combined with maturing sexuality.

Conjugal Love Stage: Idealization is replaced by the reality of living together and romantic love is replaced by years of shared experience and commitment.

Parental Love Stage: Nurturance is provided to children and aging parents.

Grandparental Love Stage: Tenderness and consideration increase in the feelings older men and women have for one another and their grandchildren.

<u>Normative Pressure to Move Through Stages</u>: Peers and others signal appropriate progress by expressing approval or disapproval.

<u>Initial Preoccupation and Indifference</u>: Total absorption is characteristic of the early phase of each developmental stage until the tasks have been mastered and cease to be of further concern.

<u>Infatuation:</u> A term which describes overwhelming, sudden attraction.

<u>Idealization:</u> The tendency to perceive the loved one more favorably than others.

<u>Romanticism and Marriage</u>: Romanticism is replaced by realism as a couple moves closer to marriage.

LEARNING OBJECTIVES

Fill in the words required to complete each sentence.

Learning Objective 1

Describe the development of love.

a. Most Americans believe love to be the __Preferred__ basis for __MARRIAGE__ .

b. In this context, love refers to the __EROTIC__ , mutually supportive, and __COOPERATIVE__ relationship of a woman and man.

c. The first __developmental__ task in the preparation for love is the establishment of a firm __gender__ identity.

d. Development of gender identity depends on a satisfactory __LOVE__ relationship with one's __PARENTS__ .

e. The next developmental task requires adjustment to teachers and __FRIENDS__ , and then to persons of the __OPPOSITE__ sex.

f. Finally, adjustment to college is followed by __COURTShip__ and __MARRAGE__ . Parenthood and __GRANDPARENT hood__ extend the developmental process into old age.

Learning Objective 2

Describe the early stages in the development of love.

a. ___INFANTS___ cannot be very active participants in love ___Relatioships___ with their parents.

b. However, infants do ___Respond___ to the ___NURTURING___ of their parents.

c. They also learn that such responses as smiling and cooing ___elicit___ atten-tion and ___Affection___ from their parents.

d. By early ___childhood___, the emotional responses of infants progress to ___Awareness___ of other people.

e. The adult role now shifts slightly from ___NURSE___ and protector to that of loving ___teacher___ .

f. The ___Opedial___ period occurs when children develop ___Sexual___ attraction to the ___PAret___ of the opposite sex.

g. Although the child immediately ___Repress___ his or her attraction, flirtations and ___Seductive___ behaviors continue to be directed toward the opposite-sex parent.

h. Understanding parents know that oedipal children are learning ___enotic___ behaviors to incorporate into later ___Affectionat___ relationships with the opposite sex.

Learning Objective 3

Describe the middle stages in the development of love.

a. In the ___Childhood___ years, peer relationships of great interpersonal ___Intamacy___ are formed.

b. Occasionally ___Cross-sex___ friendships develop into ___Intamacy___, but pre-adolescent boys and girls are usually completely dependent on ___Planned___ social ___Activitys___.

c. More often, pre-adolescents ___Rehorce___ with ___friends___ of the same sex the intimacy they will eventually share with the opposite sex.

d. ___Youth___ is the stage that fits ___between___ pre-adolescence and adoles-cence. The crucial feature of youth is overt ___Destification___ with ___Adult___ role ___modles___ of the same sex.

58

e. A second feature of this stage is the tendency of youth toward _Idealization_
    Eventually this idealization _TRANSFERS_ to _heterosexual_ relationships.

f. In the _teenAge_ years, idealization combines with the full development of
    sexual _PASSION_. Eventually _physical_ and emotional intimacy combine
    to move a couple toward _commitment_

g. Despite rapid movement toward _MARRAGE_, many couples are advised to
    de-romatisize the relationship and to view their _PARTNERS_ realistically.

Learning Objective 4

Describe the late stages in the development of love.

a. _Conjugal_ love is less exclusively _erotic_ than romantic love.

b. Conjugal love is based on a deeper _intimacy_ that develops with years of
    shared _experiences_ and great _commitment_ to one another.

c. Sex is openly shared in a context of _domestic_ cooperation, and if
    passion grows less overwhelming, _affection_ grows far more pervasive.

d. Parental love is often turned toward one's own _PARENTS_, as old age in-
    creases their _dependency_

e. Parental love of children includes _physical_, personal, and _erotic_
    nurturing, and provision of adult _Role_ models.

f. _tenderness_ becomes more prominent in the love of the elderly for each other
    and their _grandchildren_

g. Grandfathers are relieved of demands for authority and _Masculity_ that
    complicated their previous relationships. Grandmothers are relieved of the
    need to be _disiplinarians_ and they frequently _indulge_ their grandchildren.

Learning Objective 5

Describe the experiences of love and fulfillment.

a. Progress toward _emotioal_ maturity is the outcome of the kind of love that
    moves the individual on to the next developmental _stage_.

b. Most _developmental_ tasks, including those of _love_, totally
    preoccupy the individual who is involved with them.

c. Considerable preoccupation, _excitment_, and fascination mark people's _progress_ through the _stages_ of love development.

d. In general, we develop forms of _love_ which are compatible with our developmental _tasks_ .

e. Romantic love often yields to a love of _two_ people who have shared _problems_ and tragedies as well as passion.

f. Each stage of love _development_ means personal _growth_ , a process which continues throughout _life_ .

Learning Objective 6

Describe the role of love in the movement toward marriage.

a. Up to _1/3_ of _college_ women and men experience "love at first sight."

b. One school of thought opposes _infatuation_ as a basis for _marriage_. It suggests that marriages based on infatuation will lead to disillusionment and _divorce_ .

c. The outcome of infatuation is _idealization_ the _tendency_ to see the loved one more _realistic_ than others do.

d. A study with engagement _adjustment_ scales has shown that _romantic_ couples score as high as more _realistic_ couples.

e. As students grow _older_ and closer to _marriage_ they idealize their _partners_ less than before.

f. Young married couples appear to be _less_ romantic than teenagers or _older_ couples. Most couples approach mate _selection_ with a good deal of conscious _awareness_.

MULTIPLE CHOICE QUESTIONS

_b_ 1. Which of the following is <u>not</u> part of the definition of married love?

    a. erotic pleasure   c. cooperation
    b. division of labor   d. mutual support

_b_ 2. The development of ___b___ identity is crucial to later emotional growth.

    a. sexual

b.   gender
c.   ego
d.   role

___C__ 3.   The idea that certain achievements accompany specific ages leads to the con-
cept of developmental

a.   sequences.   c.   tasks.
b.   roles.   d.   identities.

___b__ 4.   The third developmental stage of love is

a.   early childhood.   c.   youth.
b.   the oedipal period.   d.   pre-adolescence.

___C__ 5.   Which stage is most characterized by overt identification with adult role
models of the same sex?

a.   early childhood   c.   youth
b.   the oedipal period   d.   pre-adolescence

___D__ 6.   Which stage is most characterized by same-sex friendships?

a.   early childhood   c.   youth
b.   the oedipal period   d.   pre-adolescence

___D__ 7.   The _____ stage shows the greatest development of sexual passion.

a.   conjugal   c.   youth
b.   parental   d.   teenage

___C__ 8.   Which is the last type of nurturing parents provide their children?

a.   personal   c.   erotic
b.   spiritual   d.   physical

___C__ 9.   Most frequently, parental love also turns toward one's own

a.   siblings.   c.   parents.
b.   employees.   d.   neighbors.

___C__ 10. In conjugal love, sex is shared more openly in a context of _____
cooperation.

a.   financial   c.   domestic
b.   physical   d.   spiritual

A 11. The most prominent characteristic of the love of the elderly is

    a. tenderness.   c. competition.
    b. passion.   d. discipline.

TRUE FALSE QUESTIONS

T 1. Developmental tasks assume that certain achievements are appropriate for different ages.

F 2. A person who fails a developmental task simply moves on to the next stage.

F 3. Early childhood is the first stage of love development.

F 4. In the oedipal period, a child develops erotic attraction to the parent of the same sex.

F 5. The pre-adolescent stage most often involves close friendships between children of the opposite sex.

T 6. The teenage stage includes the full development of sexual passion.

T 7. Conjugal love is less exclusively sexual than romantic love.

T 8. Parental love involves erotic nurturing of pre-adolescent children.

T 9. "Love at first sight" is an example of infatuation.

F 10. Young married couples are more romantic than either teenage or older married couples.

MATCHING

E 1. grandparental love   a. identification with adult role models

D 2. infancy   b. judging more favorably than others

B 3. idealization   c. development of sexual passion

C 4. teenage stage   d. total physical dependence

I 5. conjugal love   e. tender and undemanding

A 6. youth   f. awareness of other people

62

_G_ 7. oedipal period _g._ sexual attraction to parent

_A_ 8. early childhood _h._ same-sex friendship

_h_ 9. pre-adolescence _i._ shared experience and commitment

ESSAY QUESTIONS

1. Explain why men and women who are idealistic about their fiancees may score
    higher than more realistic couples on engagement adjustment scales. Provide
    an informed opinion of the most probable findings if marital adjustment scales
    were administered to these same couples a few years after marriage.

2. Explain why society looks more favorably on forms of love in which individuals
    nurture others rather than those in which individuals primarily receive love.

3. Describe the conditions that render conjugal love less exclusively sexual than
    romantic love.

4. Explain what is meant by the statement that each type of love is coordinated
    to the most important tasks of each developmental stage.

ANSWERS

Learning Objective 1

a. preferred, marriage
b. erotic, cooperative
c. developmental, gender
d. love, parents
e. schoolmates, opposite
f. courtship, marriage, grandparenthood

Learning Objective 2

a. infants, relationships
b. respond, nurturing
c. elicit, affection
d. childhood, awareness
e. nurse, teacher
f. oedipal, sexual, parent
g. represses, seductive
h. erotic, affectional

Learning Objective 3

a. childhood, intimacy
b. cross-sex, intimacy, planned, activities
c. rehearse, friends
d. youth, between, identification, adult, models
e. idealization, transfers, heterosexual
f. teenage, passion, physical, commitment
g. marriage, de-romanticize, partners

Learning Objective 4

a. conjugal, erotic
b. intimacy, experiences, commitment
c. domestic, passion, affection
d. parents, dependency
e. physical, erotic, role
f. tenderness, grandchildren
g. masculinity, complicated, disciplinarians, indulge

Learning Objective 5

a. emotional, stage
b. developmental, love, preoccupy
c. excitement, progress, stages
d. love, tasks
e. two, problems
f. development, growth, life

Learning Objective 6

a. one-third, college
b. infatuation, marriage, divorce
c. idealization, tendency, favorably
d. adjustment, romantic, realistic
e. older, marriage, partners
f. less, older, selection, awareness

MULTIPLE CHOICE QUESTIONS

1. b
2. b
3. c
4. b
5. c

6. d
7. d
8. c
9. c
10. c
11. a

TRUE FALSE QUESTIONS

1. T
2. F
3. F
4. F
5. F

6. T
7. T
8. T
9. T
10. F

MATCHING

1. e
2. d
3. b
4. c
5. i

6. a
7. g
8. f
9. h

Chapter 6

MATE SELECTION

KEY TERMS AND CONCEPTS

Prohibited Relationships: Law forbidding marriage or sexual intercourse with certain relatives.

Consanguinity Prohibitions: Prevention of marriage between "blood relatives."

Affinity Prohibitions: Prevention of marriage between people who are already related by marriage.

Blood Test: Marriage requirement in many states to test for syphilis.

Sex Ratio: The number of men per 100 women.

Homogamy: Describes the fact that most people marry partners similar to themselves.

Mating Gradient: The traditional expectation that men marry downward in age, education, and social class.

Residential Propinquity: The tendency to marry partners who live nearby.

Organizational Propinquity: Organizations involved in education, employment, recreational or civic activities, and religious services bring people together regularly in meaningful contacts that may lead to marriage.

Field of Eligibles: The total number of persons with appropriate characteristics for being considered as potential mates.

Heterogamy: Emerging tendency for people to marry partners who differ from themselves in important ways.

Religious Homogamy: Describes the fact that most people marry within their own religious group.

Interfaith Marriage and Divorce Rate: Interfaith marriages, taken as a whole, have higher divorce rates. The characteristics of those most likely to enter inter-faith marriages (older at time of marriage, higher social status, previous divorce) probably reduce the potential divorce rate.

Interracial Marriage and Divorce Rate: Couples where the husband is black and the wife is white have lower divorce rates than white couples.

Theory of Complementary Needs: The idea that marital partners are selected to fit unfulfilled personality needs.

Stimulus Stage: First attraction is based on perceptions of one's own and the other person's desirable qualities. Continuing attraction is maintained through equivalence of one's own assets and the other's assets.

Value Stage: Comparison of the compatibility of values, attitudes and feelings about children, religion, politics, and money. Greater similarity enhances the self-concept of each partner.

Role Stage: An advanced level of intimacy and reality testing in which each partner assesses how the other copes with success and failure, responsibility, daily routine, and sexual interaction.

LEARNING OBJECTIVES

Fill in the words required to complete each sentence.

Learning Objective 1

Describe the legal requirements of mate selection.

a. It isn't helpful to think of ___LOVE___ as a cause of marriage. Being in love doesn't cause long-term __Commitment__ and we need to study the ___Factors___ of mate selection.

b. The general factors of mate selection are law, place of __Residence__ , social __Characterist__ and personal ___Choice___ .

c. All states have ___LAWS___ forbidding marriage between certain __Relatives__. Over half of the states prohibit marriage between ___Fist___ cousins and half __Siblings__ . These prohibitions are based on __Consanguinty__

d. All states require that persons reach certain ___Ages___ before they __Marrie__ . The most common ages with __parental__ consent are 18 for ___Men___ and 16 for ___Women___ . Without such consent, the most common age is _____18_____ for both sexes.

e. A majority of states require a ___Blood___ test to certify that both partners are free of _Spiplls_ .

f. The most common waiting period is _____3_____ days. A substantial number of couples who __Apply__ for marriage _liccnces_ never use them.

Learning Objective 2

Describe the social principles of mate selection.

a. The sex __RATIO__ is the number of men per _____100_____ women. Rural areas have __higher__ sex ratios; urban areas have __Lower__ sex ratios.

b. Men __MARRY__ at an average age of _____23_____; women at an average of ___21___.

c. The idea that we "__MARRY__ alike" is called the principle of __homogamy__.

d. In general, we also marry those who are __Similiar__ to us in __social__ class.

e. According to the mating __gradient__ men tended to marry downward in age, __education__, and social __class__. More recent data suggest the __MATING__ gradient does not __exist__.

f. Studies of ___City___ residents have shown that about one-half of those who marry live within 20 __Blocks__ of each other. This provides evidence for the principle of residential __propinquity__

g. Recent social changes suggest that __Residential__ propinquity may be less important to mate selection than __oGazational__ propinquity.

Learning Objective 3

Describe the basic characteristics of interfaith marriage.

a. Religious __homogamy__ is still the rule, however, the situation is now changing toward __Hetegamy__ in mate __Selection__.

b. About _____91_____ percent of __College__ students are willing to marry a person of a different faith. As many as _____30_____ percent of Catholics are now marrying nonCatholics, and interfaith marriage of ___Jews___ is increasing even faster.

/

c. ___Religious___ opposition to interfaith marriage has been changing and ___weakening___.

d. Traditionally, Catholics who married nonCatholics were required to sign an ___Antinupal___ Agreement. Now the Catholic partner need only promise to ___baptise___ and ___rear___ all children in the faith.

e. ___Jews___ distinguish between two types of interfaith marriage, ___intermanng___ and ___mix___ marriage. There has been an increase in the number of ___Reformed___ rabbis willing to perform ___Mixed___ marriages.

f. ___Protisents___ oppose mixed marriages on the grounds of marital ___istability___ and fear that the couple and its _____ will not practice the specific faith.

g. Religiously ___homogamus___ marriages have lower ___Divorce___ rates than mixed marriages.

h. Couples who are ___older___ and of ___high___ social ___class___ are most likely to enter mixed marriages.

Learning Objective 4

Describe the basic characteristics of interracial marriage.

a. Pressures toward ___racial___ homogamy are stronger than those supporting ___Religious___ homogamy. A ___1967___ ruling by the United States Supreme Court has held laws against interracial marriage to be ___uncostitutional___

b. In 1977, about ___52___ percent of the population approved of black-white marriage, compared to ___29___ percent in ___1971___.

c. There were about 85,000 ___white indian___ and 55,000 ___white onentl___ marriages in 1970.

d. The majority of black-white marriages involve a ___white___ wife and ___black___ husband.

e. Black-white marriages also tend to occur among ___older___ couples, they produce relatively few ___children___, but they appear to be as ___staboel___ as other marriages.

f. Black husbands often stated that the ___hostility___ and aggressiveness of ___black___ women led them to seek ___white___ spouses.

g. Black-white couples most frequently encounter discrimination in ___employmet___ and ___housing___.

h. The _____Family_____ of the _____white_____ partner is more likely to reject the couple.

i. _____INteRacIal_____ couples seldom _____fight_____ about race.

Learning Objective 5

Describe how personality characteristics influence mate selection.

a. Many _____factors_____ of mate selection operate largely on the basis of _____chance_____.

b. Personality _____characteris_____ are most important to the final _____selection_____ process.

c. The theory of complementary _____needs_____ is based on the idea that _____Opposites_____ attract.

d. A large body of _____ResAnch_____ has _____failed_____ to support complementary theories of mate selection.

e. One problem is that personality needs are highly _____Abstract_____ and difficult to _____Measure_____.

f. A closely related problem is that people appear to marry on the basis of _____Perceved_____ rather than _____Actual_____ personality _____charactenistics_____

Learning Objective 6

Describe the stimulus-value-role theory of mate selection.

a. The stimulus stage involves the _____Assement_____ of one's own _____Attractive_____ qualities, and those of the other person.

b. Most people then _____Approach_____ members of the opposite sex to whom they feel approximately _____equal_____.

c. Both partners construct a balance _____Sheet_____ of assets and liabilities, and the next stage occurs only if the _____balance_____ is favorable to both.

d. The _____value_____ stage involves discussion of each partner's most important attitudes and _____feelings_____. High value _____similarity_____ leads to _____stronger_____ attraction because each partner receives positive _____Reinforcment_____ from the other.

e. Each partner also _____eNhancer_____ the other's _____self concept_____

70

f. The ___Role___ stage involves testing the relationship at increasing levels of ___INTAMACY___ and ___REALITY___ .

g. Most couples are ___AWARE___ of the assets and liabilities of their ___RELATIONSHIPS___, and they ___MARRY___ when the former outweigh the latter.

MULTIPLE CHOICE QUESTIONS

___C___ 1. Which of the following is <u>not</u> a factor of mate selection?

    a. law   c. love
    b. residence   d. personal choice

___D___ 2. Which of the following is <u>not</u> a legal requirement for marriage?

    a. nonconsanguinity   c. a marriage license
    b. blood test   d. financial responsibility

___C___ 3. The sex _____ is the number of men per 100 women.

    a. balance   c. ratio
    b. proportion   d. count

___A___ 4. _____ describes the finding that most people marry those who are similar to themselves.

    a. homogamy   c. monogamy
    b. heterogamy   d. complementarity

___B___ 5. The belief that men tend to marry downward in age, education, and social class assumes the existence of

    a. affirmative action.   c. polyandry.
    b. a mating gradient.   d. equal opportunity.

___A___ 6. Residential propinquity may now be a less influential factor of mate selection than _____ propinquity.

    a. organizational   c. religious
    b. political   d. ethnic

A 7. Which of the following is <u>not</u> an essential provision of the Ante-Nuptial Agreement?

    a. prohibition of extra-marital sex
    b. one wedding ceremony
    c. prohibition of birth control
    d. prohibition of divorce

C 8. Which of the following is <u>not</u> a branch of Judaism?

    a. Reform
    b. Conservative
    c. Traditional
    d. Orthodox

d 9. Which of the following variables is <u>not</u> known to be associated with the probability of an interfaith marriage?

    a. age of the couple
    b. social class
    c. previous divorce
    d. personality needs

C 10. In 1970, the most frequent type of interracial marriage was between

    a. blacks and whites.
    b. whites and Japanese.
    c. whites and Indians.
    d. blacks and Japanese.

b 11. Compared to racially homogamous marriages, black-white marriages are more likely to

    a. involve younger couples.
    b. produce fewer children.
    c. terminate in divorce.
    d. involve sexually inexperienced couples.

A 12. Black-white couples are <u>least</u> likely to quarrel about

    a. race.
    b. finances.
    c. domestic responsibilities.
    d. personality differences.

A 13. The belief that people select partners who meet their unfilled personality needs is the theory of _____ needs.

    a. complementary
    b. similar
    c. differential
    d. reciprocal

B 14. Couples are most likely to <u>assess their</u> own <u>attractive qualities</u> and <u>those of others</u> during the

    a. role stage.
    b. stimulus stage.
    c. sexual stage.
    d. value stage.

_d_ 15. Couples are most likely to discuss their attitudes and deepest feelings during the

    a. role stage.   c. sexual stage.
    b. stimulus stage.   d. value stage.

_A_ 16. Couples test their relationships at increasing levels of intimacy and reality during the

    a. role stage.   c. sexual stage.
    b. stimulus stage.   d. value stage.

_b_ 17. In the schematic summary of mate selection, each process is presented as a series of

    a. obstacles.   c. opportunities.
    b. filters.   d. assets and liabilities.

TRUE FALSE QUESTIONS

_T_ 1. All states have laws forbidding marriage with certain relatives.

_F_ 2. A majority of states permit marriage between first cousins.

_F_ 3. The sex ratio is the number of women per 100 men.

_T_ 4. The principle of homogamy states that we marry those who are similar to us.

_F_ 5. Residential propinquity is replacing organizational propinquity as a factor of mate selection.

_T_ 6. Interfaith marriage is an example of heterogamous mate selection.

_F_ 7. When a Protestant marries a nonProtestant, both parties must sign an Ante-Nuptial Agreement.

_F_ 8. Interracial marriage is more common than interreligious marriage.

_T_ 9. Public attitudes are more accepting of interreligious marriage than of interracial marriage.

_T_ 10. Chance is one of the most important factors in mate selection.

_F_ 11. The theory of complementary needs is based on the idea that like attracts like.

___T___ 12. Partners typically discuss their attitudes and feelings during the value stage. *T*

___F___ 13. A relationship is tested for intimacy and reality during the stimulus stage. *F*

___T___ 14. Most couples assess the assets and liabilities of their relationship before they marry. *T*

MATCHING

___C___ 1. consanguinity *C*   a. number of prospective mates

___D___ 2. sex ratio *D*   b. intimacy and reality testing

___e___ 3. homogamy *e*   c. blood relationship

___i___ 4. mating gradient *i*   d. higher in rural areas

___J___ 5. propinquity *J*   e. like marries like

___A___ 6. field of eligibles *A*   f. sharing attitudes and feelings

___G___ 7. heterogamy *G*   g. marriage outside one's group

___K___ 8. complementary needs *K*   h. assessment of attractive qualities

___h___ 9. stimulus stage *h*   i. men marry downward

___D___ 10. role stage *b*   j. physical proximity

___A___ 11. value stage *f*   k. opposites attract

ESSAY QUESTIONS

1. Explain why American marriages tend to be homogamous in age, religion, race, social class, income, education, political beliefs, values, attitudes, and personality traits. Describe some additional determinants of mate selection which are either homogamous or heterogamous.

2. Explain why traditional attitudes toward men and women supported the idea of a mating gradient. As women increase their opportunities for education, political power, and income, is it possible that a reverse mating gradient will occur?

3. Describe the different types of organizational propinquity that are replacing residential propinquity as an important factor of mate selection.

ANSWERS

Learning Objective 1

a. love, commitment, factors
b. residence, characteristics, choice
c. laws, relatives, first, siblings, consanguinity
d. ages, marry, parental, men, women, 18
e. blood, syphilis
f. three, apply, licenses

Learning Objective 2

a. ratio, 100, higher, lower
b. marry, 23, 21
c. marry, homogamy
d. similar, social
e. gradient, education, class, mating, exist
f. city, blocks, propinquity
g. residential, organizational

Learning Objective 3

a. homogamy, heterogamy, selection
b. 91, college, 30, Jews
c. religious, weakening
d. Ante-Nuptial, baptize, rear
e. Jews, intermarriage, mixed, Reform, mixed
f. Protestants, instability,
g. homogamous, divorce
h. older, higher, class

Learning Objective 4

a. racial, religious, 1967, unconstitutional
b. 52, 29, 1971
c. white-indian, white-oriental
d. white, black
e. older, children, stable
f. hostility, black, white
g. employment, housing
h. family, white
i. interracial, fight

Learning Objective 5

a. factors, chance
b. characteristics, selection
c. needs, opposites
d. research, failed
e. abstract, measure
f. perceived, actual, characteristics

Learning Objective 6

a. assessment, attractive
b. approach, equal
c. sheet, balance
d. value, feelings, similarity, stronger, reinforcement
e. enhances, self-concept
f. role, intimacy, reality
g. aware, relationships, marry

MULTIPLE CHOICE QUESTIONS

1. c
2. d
3. c
4. a
5. b
6. a
7. a
8. c
9   d

10. c
11. b
12. a
13. a
14. b
15. d
16. a
17. b

TRUE FALSE QUESTIONS

1. T
2. F
3. F
4. T
5. F
6. T
7. F

8. F
9. T
10. T
11. F
12. T
13. F
14. T

MATCHING

1.	c	7.	g
2.	d	8.	k
3.	e	9.	h
4.	i	10.	b
5.	j	11.	f
6.	a		

Chapter 7

LEARNING TO LIVE TOGETHER

KEY TERMS AND CONCEPTS

<u>Women's Role Expectations</u>: The attitudes and beliefs women bring to their enactmen.
of adult behavior as determined by primary and secondary socialization.

<u>Career Oriented</u>: Women who plan for a career.

<u>Non-Career Oriented</u>: Women who plan toward traditional homemaking activities and
traditional female occupations.

<u>Converts</u>: Women without career aspirations but who develop them during the college
years.

<u>Shifters</u>: Women who vacillate between career and noncareer orientations.

<u>Defectors</u>: Women who move from career to homemaking interests during college.

<u>Equalitarianism</u>: Women sharing equally with their husband the worlds of work and
home.

<u>Traditionalist Males</u>: Men who intend to marry women who would not seek employment.

<u>Modified Traditionalist Males</u>: Men who believe their wives might work before
children are born and after they are grown.

<u>Pseudo-Feminist Males</u>: Men who are willing to have their wives work as long as
they are not inconvenienced.

<u>Feminist Males</u>: Men who are willing to make changes in their own roles so their
wives can pursue careers.

<u>Counterculture</u>: Women and men who wish people to relate to one another spontaneously
and freely, seeking intimacy, naturalness, and unrestrained satisfaction.

"Psychology of Plenty:" An attitude which emphasizes absence of worry about finding love and financial security.

Marriage Contracts: An agreement between a couple which describes the rights and duties of each partner.

Legal Status of Marriage: State control of who may enter marriage, conditions within marriage, and conditions for dissolving marriage.

Dower Rights: Common-law rights which define a wife's entitlement to one-third to one-half of the couple's home.

Community Property Laws: Laws which entitle a wife to one-half interest in all property acquired by a couple during their marriage.

Constructive Use of Marriage Contracts: An agreement for approaching marriage with a firmer sense of reality.

Disillusionment: Recognition early in marriage that one's spouse cannot meet all of one's needs all of the time.

Acute Quarrels: Quarrels that occur as part of learning to live together.

Progressive Quarrels: Quarrels that miss the issues and focus on personalities, thus inflicting considerable damage.

Habituated Quarrels: Areas where agreement can never be reached and are avoided most of the time.

Insight: Understanding the underlying motives of one's partner and oneself.

Power Relationships: Dominance that allows one partner of a relationship to make the greater number of important decisions.

Husband-Dominant Pattern: The husband manages the marital relationship.

Syncratic Pattern: Decision-making is equal and shared.

Autonomic Pattern: Decision-making is equal but many decisions are made independently of the partner.

LEARNING OBJECTIVES

Fill in the words required to complete each sentence.

Learning Objective 1

Describe recent changes in women's role expectations for marriage.

a. Many College-Educ women question the adequacy of marriage as a source of
    life Fullfilment. They are stimulated to develop Occupational as well as
    family goals.

b. Early studies showed that CAReeR women began dATiN at later ages,
    enjoyed Children less, and least enjoyed domestic activities.

c. Compared to traditional women, career-oriented women were more likely to have
    working Mothers, were influenced more by professors than by peers and
    family, and they had worked at more Job's while in college.

d. The five work types among college women are NOCAREeRsT, converts,
    Careenist, shifters, and defectors. According to these data about
    half of today's college women have serious CAReeR interests.

e. About 79 percent of senior women most prefer the future role of married
    working woman with children.

f. More women want to be full partners with their husbands in the world of
    work and they want their husbands to be full partners in the
    home.

Learning Objective 2

Describe the changes in men's role expectations for their wives.

a. On the basis of their attitudes toward their future wives' employment, college
    men were divided into four categories: traditionalists, modified tradition-
    alists, persedo fem, and feminists.

b. Tradftbo were confident of their ability to support their families and they
    intended to marry women who would not work.

c. Modified traditionalists believed that youns children needed their
    mothers at home.

d. Pseudo-feminists approved of maternal employment in the __ABSTRACT__ . However, they were inclined to impose __CoNDITIONS__ that few women could __FulFill__ .

e. Men classified as feminists were willing to make any __CHANGES__ short of a complete reversal of __Roles__ .

f. A recent comparison of men's and women's sex-role __OXPECTATION__ showed greatest consensus about __FAMialy__ roles and most disagreement over __OCUUPATIONAl__ roles.

Learning Objective 3

Describe the influence of the counterculture on men's and women's marital roles.

a. In a recent investigation, about __80%__ of a total of two thousand marriages were classified as __CounterCult__ marriages. Most such marriages were on the east and west __COASTS__ .

b. There was considerable __UCONVETiON__ in the __Roles__ played by men and women.

c. Counterculture couples appear to be more __SexuAlly__ active than most couples their age, but they also seem less __preocupid__ with sex.

d. A third characteristic of these marriages is that couples did not seek to __MiNiMEe__ tension. __ConFlict__ was a valued part of the interaction of specific couples' __problem Solving__

e. Finally, counterculture couples seem to place little emphasis on getting ahead __FiNACiAlly__

f. Over time, these marriages showed a __TREND__ to revert to more __Convetion al__ patterns.

Learning Objective 4

Describe several important characteristics of marriage contracts.

a. A marriage contract is a __Sised__ document in which husband and wife specify their respective __Rights__ and __obligation__ in marriage. The current __obligation__ in such contracts is part of an effort to make marriage more personally __meAuts R.|__

b. Marriage is a legal __STAtus__ , controlled by the __STAtY__ . The defini-tions of this status are descended from __traditional__ common __LAW__ .

c. Basically, this law obligates husbands to provide _finacial_ support. In return, they are entitled to the wife's _companioship_ and to sexual _intercourse_.

d. Legal requirements are important to a marriage contract, because the _state_ will not _enforce_ any agreement that is not consistent with them.

e. In states where _common_ law prevails, wives have _dower_ right in their husbands' property. In states with _community_ property laws, the wife has a _half inmst_ in all property acquired during the marriage.

f. Couples may enter agreements that do not interfere with the rights and obligations of the partners under either _common_ law or _statuer_ law. All other agreements are legally _void_ .

g. Good marriages are built upon _love_ , trust, and _unselfisness_, not on precise statements of _rights_ and _duties_ .

Learning Objective 5

Describe the basic characteristics of initial marital adjustments.

a. Couples who really come to know each other before _marrise_ may experience little or no _disillusionment_

b. The most _threatnig_ aspect of disillusionment is the implication of personal _rejection_ .

c. In one study of 385 parental couples, _16_ percent were reported to have engaged in _physical_ violence during the preceding year.

d. A recent study of conflict in marriage classified couples into four types: screaming sluggers, _silent_ attackers, threateners, and _pacifists_ .

e. Marital _quarrels_ may be classified in terms of three types: _acute_ , progressive, and _habitual_ .

f. Acute quarrels grow out of the need to establish a _succeeful_ modus _operadi_ .

g. Progressive quarrels occur when couples fail to resolve the _issues_ and focus on each other's _personality_ instead.

h. Habituated conflict remains after couples have worked out their basic _adjustments_ and learned to avoid _progressive_ conflict.

Learning Objective 6

Describe the role of insight in effective marital communication.

a. Insight is the __CAPACITY__ to understand the __MOTIVATIONS__ for one's partner's behavior and for one's own.

b. Insightful people realize that attacks by the partner are usually motivated out of __hurt__ or fear, __Rejection__, or fear of __Retaliation__.

c. Possession of __power__ and insight are __inversly__ related.

d. The trend toward more __equality__ in marriage may be encouraging a more equal __distribution__ of insight.

e. Insight is __ethically__ neutral; it may be used to further __sharing__ and love or in __exploitative__ manipulation.

f. A recent study on marital communication revealed four styles of openness and disclosure: conventional, __speculative__, controlling, and __contactul__.

g. The __Convetioal__ style is both closed and nondisclosing, but the __contactul__ style is both open and highly disclosing.

Learning Objective 7

Describe the basic patterns of power in marital relationships.

a. Differential __distributio__ of power is a feature of all __Relationships__. Adult interaction gradually evolves to an __Male__ dominance-submission __informal__ in which some people lead and others follow.

b. There are three basic marital power patterns: __Male__ domination, __Female__ domination, and __equality__.

c. We are now moving in the direction of more __equalitarian__ relationships and fewer __Ausband__ dominated ones.

d. In a recent Los Angeles study of power, respondents' answers classified their relationships into one of four patterns: husband-dominated, __Sycnatic__, wife-dominated, and __Autonomul__.

e. The most frequently occurring power pattern was the __Automatic__, while the least common pattern was the __wifedominat__

f. Greatest __manital__ satisfaction was reported by couples in the __Automatic__ pattern, and least satisfaction among couples in the __wifedomuate__ pattern.

84

g. Other studies show that ___shared___ power is associated with good
___health___, the wife's ___employment___, and greater ___flexibilty___ in coping
with crises.

MULTIPLE CHOICE QUESTIONS

__B__ 1. Which of the following is <u>not</u> part of the traditional stereotype of women
who pursued masculine occupations?

    a. poor marital risk   c. dislike of children
    b. high sex drive   d. less frequent dating

__B__ 2. Compared to more traditional women, those who sought entry into masculine
professions

    a. had more mothers who did not work.
    b. had worked at more jobs during college.
    c. were more influenced by peers and family than by professors and pro-
        fessionals.
    d. were more likely to report lesbian tendencies.

__D__ 3. In a New York study which asked senior co-eds to imagine their most desirable life styles, the majority of women

    a. chose to remain childless.
    b. chose marriage and a career without children.
    c. chose marriage and children without a career.
    d. chose marriage, careers, and children.

__C__ 4. In a recent study of counterculture marriages, it was found that most
couples

    a. completely reversed their sex roles.
    b. were preoccupied with sex.
    c. cultivated tension for problem-solving.
    d. felt insecure about money and other relationships.

__B__ 5. Over time, these counterculture marriages

    a. became even more radical.   c. remained about the same.
    b. became more conventional.   d. terminated in divorce.

__C__ 6. In return for support of his wife, a husband is legally entitled to

    a. emotional support.   c. companionship and sexual intercourse.
    b. children.   d. aid, comfort, and nurturing.

A   7. _____ property legislation grants the wife one-half interest in
all property acquired during the marriage.

    a. community   c. dower
    b. common   d. equalitarian

b   8. The value of a marriage contract lies in its power to

    a. provide legal protection.
    b. clarify expectations.
    c. rehearse the real disagreements which occur after marriage.
    d. enforce terms for terminating the marriage.

b   9. Which of the following is not covered by the sample marriage contract
reported in the text?

    a. family planning   c. division of labor
    b. religious participation d. domicile

b   10. The disillusionment of early marriage

    a. occurs during the honeymoon.
    b. is inversely proportional to how well the couple knows each other.
    c. dissipates along with the symptoms which give rise to it.
    d. is most frequently caused by sexual incompatibility.

b   11. From reports of their teenage children, it is estimated that _____
percent of married couples engaged in physical violence in the past year.

    a. six   c. twenty-six
    b. sixteen   d. thirty-six

C   12. For several decades, American couples have been moving slowly toward

    a. male-dominated marriages.
    b. female-dominated marriages.
    c. equalitarian marriages.
    d. authoritarian marriages.

C   13. Areas in which a couple will probably never achieve agreement lead to
_____ quarrels.

    a. acute   c. habituated
    b. progressive   d. chronic

__A__ 14. When the details of daily living need to be worked out, the result is an
_____ quarrel.

    (a.) acute   c. habituated
    b. progressive   d. chronic

__b__ 15. When issues become lost and personalities are attacked, a couple is experiencing a _____ quarrel.

    a. acute   c. habituated
    (b.) progressive   d. chronic

__C__ 16. Recent attitude surveys of college men and women suggest that the most
serious problems in future marriages will involve

    a. sexual incompatibility   (c.) maternal employment.
    b. financial sharing.   d. housing preferences.

TRUE FALSE QUESTIONS

__F__ 1. According to the state, marriage is a legal contract.

__F__ 2. Compared to more traditional women, career-oriented women were more likely
to have unemployed mothers.

__F__ 3. College men and women express very similar attitudes with respect to
maternal employment.

__F__ 4. A study of counterculture couples found that husbands and wives practiced
virtually complete sex-role reversal.

__T__ 5. Counterculture marriages appear to become more conventional with the
passage of time.

__F__ 6. The most important function of a marriage contract is to provide legal
protection for each spouse in the case of divorce.

__F__ 7. Acute quarrels result when couples fight over their own personalities
rather than the issues.

__T__ 8. Habituated conflict results from certain areas in which the couple is
unlikely to ever reach agreement.

__F__ 9. Possession of power and insight are directly related.

_F_ 10. Although such relationships are quite scarce, couples in wife-dominated marriages report greater marital satisfaction than couples in husband-dominated marriages.

MATCHING

_j_ 1. converts

_g_ 2. counterculture

_f_ 3. marriage contract

_c_ 4. legal status

_a_ 5. disillusionment

_d_ 6. acute quarrels

_h_ 7. habituated quarrels

_k_ 8. progressive quarrels

_b_ 9. insight

_i_ 10. communication styles

_e_ 11. syncratic

a. directly proportional to unreality

b. inversely proportional to power

c. controlled by the state

d. details of daily living

e. equal and shared decisions

f. statement of rights and obligations

g. freedom in all areas of life

h. agreement will never come

i. speculative and contactful

j. developed career aspirations

k. focus on personalities instead of issues

ESSAY QUESTIONS

1. Explain why wife-dominated marriages are the least common and least satisfying of all marital power relationships.

2. At present, virtually nothing is known about the marital satisfactions and divorce rates of couples who use marriage contracts. Devise a research project that might be executed in order to shed some light on this question.

3. Describe the social conditions that lead counterculture marriages to greater conventionality with the passage of time.

4. Explain why the state will not enforce the provisions of a contract which contravene the rights and obligations of the legal status of marriage.

ANSWERS

Learning Objective 1

a. college-educated, fulfillment, occupational
b. career, dating, children
c. mothers, professors, jobs
d. non-careerists, careerists, defectors, half, career
e. working, children
f. work, home

Learning Objective 2

a. modified, pseudo-feminists
b. traditionalists, work
c. young, home
d. abstract, conditions, fulfill
e. changes, roles
f. expectations, familial, occupational

Learning Objective 3

a. 80, counterculture, coasts
b. unconventionality, roles
c. sexually, preoccupied
d. minimize, conflict, problem-solving
e. financially
f. trend, conventional

Learning Objective 4

a. signed, rights, obligations, interest, meaningful
b. status, state, traditional, law
c. financial, companionship, intercourse
d. state, enforce
e. common, dower, community, half-interest
f. common, statute, void
g. love, unselfishness, rights, duties

Learning Objective 5

a. marriage, disillusionment

b. threatening, rejection
c. 16, physical
d. silent, pacifists
e. quarrels, acute, habituated
f. successful, operandi
g. issues, personalities
h. adjustments, progressive

Learning Objective 6

a. capacity, motivations
b. hurt, retaliation, rejection
c. power, inversely
d. equality, distribution
e. ethically, sharing, exploitative
f. speculative, contactful
g. conventional, contactful

Learning Objective 7

a. distribution, relationships, informal, hierarchy
b. male, female, equality
c. equalitarian, husband
d. syncratic, autonomic
e. autonomic, wife-dominant
f. marital, autonomic, wife-dominant
g. shared, health, employment, flexibility

MULTIPLE CHOICE QUESTIONS

1.	b	9.	b
2.	b	10.	b
3.	d	11.	b
4.	c	12.	c
5.	b	13.	c
6.	c	14.	a
7.	a	15.	b
8.	b	16.	c

TRUE FALSE QUESTIONS

1.	F		6.	F
2.	F		7.	F
3.	F		8.	T
4.	F		9.	F
5.	T		10.	F

MATCHING

1.	j		6.	d
2.	g		7.	h
3.	f		8.	k
4.	c		9.	b
5.	a		10.	i
			11.	e

Chapter 8

IN-LAW RELATIONSHIPS

KEY TERMS AND CONCEPTS

Similarity of Background: Intended spouses are of similar socio-economic status, education, religion, nationality, and life style.

Life Chances: Probability of a desirable standard of living for one's self and children.

Unresolved Dependency: The anticipated loss of their children's dependency arouses parental fear and anxiety.

Loss of Parental Role: Anxiety created by the loss of the parental role when one's children marry.

Couple Solidarity: A sense of belonging to a unit whose members put obligations to each other before obligations to others.

Adversary Relationship: A situation in which parents and their offspring and spouse are in conflict.

Parental Support: Aid to the young married couple which may include tuition, money, furniture, food, trips, or services.

LEARNING OBJECTIVES

Fill in the words required to complete each sentence.

Learning Objective 1

Describe in-law relationships during the early pre-marital period.

a. One partner may know the other's _____ long before _____ interest develops.

b. Most couples want to remain close to their _____ and want their parents to _____ of their intended spouses.

c. A prospective spouse of a similar _____ and occupational _____ will be welcomed most quickly.

d. Parents may also be interested in _____ background, and _____.

e. One price for marrying a very _____ partner is the sacrifice of some _____ to one's own family.

f. The parents' _____ reactions are likely to be most favorable if the prospective partner fits their _____ of a helpful _____.

Learning Objective 2

Describe in-law relationships when couples live together.

a. Many parents precipitate a _____ when they first learn of their children's _____ relationships.

b. When couples live together, the _____ parents are less often a source of _____. Parents may acknowledge their sons' need for _____, but they may then attack the young woman for being _____.

c. A living-together situation is usually more _____ for the _____ parents.

d. The young woman is likely to be more _____ to her parents' _____.

e. Young people are not likely to stop living together simply because it _____ their _____ with their parents.

f. Couples who live together in _____ of their parents must expect _____.

Learning Objective 3

Describe the kinds of threats marital relationships pose to the couples' parents.

a. Some parents have strong needs to keep their children _____ on them beyond an _____ age.

b. The real fear of such parents is the _____ of the child's _____ and dependence through marriage.

c. For many parents, the prospective _____ of their children signals the approach of _____ age.

d. _____ statuses are more closely linked to _____ attractiveness, and their _____ roles are less likely to _____ for the loss of children.

e. Another problem is that marriage of the child means _____ of the parental _____.

f. The mother who does not work outside the _____ and who has focused her life around _____ will be the most _____ to loss of the parental role.

Learning Objective 4

Describe ways of handling problems between young marrieds and their in-laws.

a. More _____ and intimate _____ between young marrieds and in-laws may resolve some problems.

b. Close association often forces all the parties to interact in _____ terms, rather than in terms of _____.

c. _____ couple _____ is another effective technique for handling in-law problems.

d. This solidarity informs parents they cannot deal with their son or daughter in _____, but must now deal with the couple as a _____.

e. Another solution is for the young couple to act more _____ than their _____.

f. For example, the couple may delay the _____ for a while in order to begin the _____ with a greater degree of parental _____.

Learning Objective 5

Describe the couple's initial marital adjustments to their in-laws.

a. Parents often _____ substantial _____ support to young married couples.

b. Wise parents structure their _____ of the young marriage so that it does not imply _____.

c. The couple's obligations for parental support are more often _____ than _____.

d. Most couples agree that neither set of _____ should be _____ over the other.

e. Adjustments between young couples and their parents must be analyzed from _____ separate _____.

f. Parents may be _____ about the withdrawal of their offspring, but they usually _____ with it.

Learning Objective 6

Describe the impact of parenthood on the relationships between married couples and their in-laws.

a. A _____ serves as an increasingly obvious symbol of the _____ of a young marriage.

b. _____ to the child now take _____ over responsibilities to the parents.

c. Relationships between the new parents and the grandparents are likely to become more _____ and more genuinely _____.

d. The grandmother is permitted to care for the new _____ while she recovers from _____.

e. The grandfather is also readily _____, but he is not really thought to be of much _____.

f. Grandfathers are allowed an openness of affection and _____ toward their _____ that is excluded from virtually every other aspect of the _____ role.

MULTIPLE CHOICE QUESTIONS

_____1. Good relationships with in-laws are more likely if the couple have

    a. similar backgrounds.   c. already lived together.
    b. dissimilar backgrounds.   d. experienced pre-marital sexual inter-
                                      course.

_____2. When a couple is sleeping together or living together,

    a. the man's parents are more likely to object.
    b. the woman's parents are more likely to object.

c. both sets of parents are equally likely to object.

d. both sets of parents usually approve of the arrangement.

_____3. Many parents believe that their daughter's _____ will be closely linked to her husband's success.

a. rate of consumption   c. sexual gratification
b. standard of living   d. marital satisfaction

_____4. Which of the following characteristics of the pre-marital situation is least likely to pose a serious threat to the parents?

a. unresolved dependency
b. recognition of aging
c. a loss of parental roles
d. a loss of financial control

_____5. Compared to middle-aged men, the statuses of middle-aged women are more closely tied to physical

a. attractiveness.   c. dexterity.
b. strength.   d. health.

_____6. With respect to loss of the parental role,

a. the father is more likely to be affected.
b. the mother is more likely to be affected.
c. both the mother and father are about equally likely to be affected.
d. both parents welcome the end of further responsibility.

_____7. Which of the following is not a recommended technique for handling problems between young married couples and their in-laws?

a. developing techniques of confrontation
b. developing couple solidarity
c. increasing contacts
d. developing understanding

_____8. Increasing contacts force all parties to interact in terms of personality rather than in terms of

a. prejudices.   c. preconceptions.
b. stereotypes.   d. first impressions.

_____9.   Couples are most likely to share their honeymoons with

     a.   their brothers and sisters.
     b.   their parents.
     c.   their wedding attendants.
     d.   their closest friends.

_____10. Parental support for the young couple is most often

     a.   social.   c.   financial.
     b.   emotional.   d.   moral.

_____11. In return for such support, the couple most frequently incurs _____ obligations to the parents.

     a.   social.   c.   financial
     b.   emotional   d.   moral

_____12. Most couples tend to favor

     a.   the husband's parents.
     b.   the wife's parents.
     c.   both sets of parents equally.
     d.   their siblings more than their in-laws.

_____13. Parents are most typically _____ about their gradual withdrawal from the lives of their children.

     a.   happy   c.   neutral
     b.   disappointed   d.   ambivalent

_____14. Arrival of a baby frequently serves to increase the _____ of the young couple.

     a.   mobility   c.   mutuality
     b.   mortality   d.   solidarity

TRUE FALSE QUESTIONS

_____1.   Parents are more likely to approve of a prospective spouse whose background is similar to their child's.

_____2.   When a couple live together, the woman's parents are more likely to object.

_____3.   It is very difficult for a couple to equalize their treatment of both sets of parents.

_____ 4. The birth of a baby tends to increase parental reservations about the son-in-law or daughter-in-law.

_____ 5. As their children prepare to marry, most in-laws welcome their withdrawal from the parental role.

_____ 6. The mother is more likely than the father to be concerned about loss of the parental role.

_____ 7. Decreasing contacts is an effective technique for handling in-law problems.

_____ 8. Increasing marital solidarity informs parents they must now deal with the couple as a unit.

_____ 9. The young married couple most frequently incurs social obligations in return for its parents' support.

_____ 10. Pregnancy and childbearing seldom alter established relationships between young couples and their parents.

MATCHING

_____ 1. similarity of background

_____ 2. living together

_____ 3. threats to parents

_____ 4. loss of parental role

_____ 5. increasing contacts

_____ 6. couple solidarity

_____ 7. parental support

_____ 8. grandchild

a. dependency, aging, and loss of role

b. more personal interaction

c. woman's parents object

d. couple must be treated as a unit

e. ends reservations about child's spouse

f. facilitates parental approval

g. entails social obligations

h. more problematic for mother

ESSAY QUESTIONS

1. Explain why parents use different criteria to evaluate a prospective son-in-law or daughter-in-law. How are young men and women likely to respond to the knowledge that their parents are using different standards of evaluation for each sex?

2. Explain why parents are so likely to value similarity of background in their children's prospective spouses.

3. Describe the threats that are posed to parents by their children's marriages and explain what techniques the children can use to help parents work through their feelings.

4. Describe the changing values of marriage that increasingly lead young couples to weary of the ritual of spending so much leisure time with their parents.

ANSWERS

Learning Objective 1

a. parents, romantic
b. families, approve
c. financial, background
d. religious, nationality
e. different, closeness
f. initial, image, spouse

Learning Objective 2

a. crisis, sexual
b. man's, trouble, sex, immoral
c. difficult, woman's
d. vulnerable, condemnation
e. prejudices, relationships
f. defiance, problems

Learning Objective 3

a. dependent, appropriate
b. loss, love
c. marriage, old
d. women's, physical, occupational, compensate
e. loss, role
f. home, child-rearing, vulnerable

Learning Objective 4

a. frequent, contacts
b. personal, stereotypes
c. developing, solidarity
d. isolation, unit
e. maturely, parents
f. wedding, marriage, approval

Learning Objective 5

a. provide, financial
b. support, dependence

c. social, financial
d. parents, favored
e. two, viewpoints
f. ambivalent, cooperate

Learning Objective 6

a. baby, solidarity
b. obligations, precedence
c. tolerant, accepting
d. mother, childbirth
e. accepted, help
f. tenderness, grandchildren, masculine

MULTIPLE CHOICE QUESTIONS

1. a
2. b
3. b
4. d
5. a
6. b
7. a

8. b
9. b
10. c
11. a
12. c
13. d
14. d

TRUE FALSE QUESTIONS

1. T
2. T
3. F
4. F
5. F

6. T
7. F
8. T
9. T
10. F

MATCHING

1. f
2. c
3. a
4. h
5. b

6. d
7. g
8. e

Chapter 9

SEXUAL ADJUSTMENT

KEY TERMS AND CONCEPTS

Penis: Cylindrical male organ which becomes erect during sexual excitement, increasing in size to roughly six inches.

Scrotum: The loose pouch of skin at the base of the. penis which holds the testicles.

Testicles: Contain tubules which continuously produce sperm cells.

Sperm Cells: The male sex cells found in numbers of over 200 million following ejaculation.

Epididymis: Twenty-foot wound tube holding maturing sperm cells.

Vas Deferens: An 18-inch tube which routes the sperm from the epididymis to the seminal vesicles.

Seminal Vesicles: Storage site for mature sperm.

Prostate: Secretes the seminal fluid that emerges during ejaculation.

Cowper's Glands: Secrete an alkaline fluid that lubricates the urethra.

Urethra: The canal which carries urine and seminal fluid.

Ovaries: Producers of the ova or eggs.

Follicles: About 10,000 small cavities on each ovary, each containing an immature ovum.

Ovulation: The mature ovum travels from the ovary to the fallopian tube.

Fallopian tube: Area where fertilization usually occurs.

Uterus: An organ in which the fertilized egg is implanted.

Vagina: A muscular tube that envelops the penis during intercourse.

Hymen: A tissue which partly obstructs the entrance to the vagina.

Vulva: The external female genitalia, including the mons veneris, the labia majora, the labia minora, the vestibule, and the clitoris.

Mons Veneris: The area above the vagina covered with hair and fatty tissue over the pubic bone.

Labia Majora: Fatty folds which enclose the vaginal opening.

Labia Minora: Folds within the labia majora provided with blood vessels and nerve endings.

Vestibule: An area enclosed by the labia minora which contains the vaginal opening and the urethra.

Clitoris: A small structure less than an inch long at the top of the vestibule. During sexual excitement it becomes engorged with blood.

Excitement Stage: Male--an erection with an increase in heart rate, blood pressure, and muscular tension. Female-- erection of nipples and clitoris, swelling of breasts and labia minora, uterine contraction and expansion, lubrication, dilation, and lengthening of the vagina.

Plateau Stage: Male and Female--a level of arousal just before orgasm.

Orgasmic Stage: Male--Involuntary contractions at the base of the penis and around the anus produce ejaculation. Female--strong involuntary contractions of the outer one-third of the vagina, uterus, perineum, rectum, and lower abdomen.

Resolution Stage: Male--loss of erection and a refractory period. Female--a decrease in muscular tension; no counterpart to the male refractory period.

Extramarital Affair: A sexual involvement of one partner with someone outside the marital bond.

Cross-Sex Friendship: Friendships with the opposite sex which may threaten the married with outside sexual involvement.

Swinging: A joint participation of the husband and wife in sexual activity with others.

LEARNING OBJECTIVES

Fill in the words required to complete each sentence.

Learning Objective 1

Describe the basic features of the male reproductive system.

a. The penis is roughly _____6_____ inches long in _____erect_____. There is no relationship between the _____size_____ of the penis and the _____sexual_____ pleasure of the man or woman.

b. The penis is composed chiefly of _____spongy_____ tissue. During sexual _____Arosal_____ this tissue fills with blood, causing an _____erection_____.

c. Consistent failure to attain or sustain an erection is called _____impotence_____ and it indicates a need for medical attention or _____pyshological_____ counseling.

d. The _____testicales_____ hang below the penis in a loose pouch of skin called the _____scrotum_____.

e. The male _____Repoductve_____ cells are called _____sperm_____.

f. Sperm are transported first to the _____epidermis_____, then to the _____vas_____ deferens, and finally to the seminal _____vestical_____.

g. Finally, sperm pass by the _____prostate_____ gland and the _____copers_____ glands before leaving the body during _____orgasm_____.

Learning Objective 2

Describe the basic characteristics of the female reproductive system.

a. The female sexual _____orgaNs_____ are primarily _____internal_____.

b. They consist of the ovaries, the fallopian _____tubes_____, the uterus, and the _____vagina_____.

c. At puberty, there are approximately 10,000 _____follicals_____ on each _____ovam_____.

d. The lower end of the uterus is called the _____cervix_____.

e. Many human societies have had _____taboos_____ about sexual intercourse during _____menstation_____.

104

f. The cervix extends into the ___upper___ end of the ___vagina___, however,
the vagina contains very few ___nerve___ endings.

g. The external female genitalia are collectively called the ___vulva___, which
consists of the mons veneris, the vestibule, the labia ___major___, the labia
___minor___, and the _____.

h. The ___clitoris___ is the most sexually excitable area of all. The head of the
clitoris is called the ___glans___.

Learning Objective 3

Describe the different stages of the male sexual response.

a. Masters and ___Johnson___ have described the sexual response in terms of
four stages: excitement, ___plateu___, orgasm, and ___resolution___

b. In men, the primary erogenous ___zone___ is the ___penis___. Additional
areas of great sensitivity to stimulation are the ___perineum___, and the
___scrotum___.

c. In the ___exicment___ stage, men experience either ___reflex___ or ___(enibit)___
erections of their penises.

d. ___Few___ definite changes occur during the ___plateu___ stage.

e. Continued ___stimulation___ at the plateau stage almost always produces
___orgasm___. Orgasm involves involuntary muscular ___contraction___, a doubling
of ___heartbeat___, and ___blood___ pressure and respiration also increase
markedly.

f. The ___resolution___ stage involves a ___refactory___ period during which men cannot
attain another ___erection___.

Learning Objective 4

Describe the different stages of the female sexual response.

a. For women, the ___clitoris___ is the primary organ, but erogenous zones are more
widespread than in ___men___.

b. The ___excitment___ stage is characterized by erection of the clitoris and
___nipples___. The labia ___majora___ also begin to ___elarge___.

c. In the ___plateu___ stage, the ___clitoris___ withdraws deeply beneath the hood
of the labia ___minora___. Just prior to ___orgasm___, the length of the

clitoris may _decrease_ by about one-half.

d. The onset of ___orgasm___ is accompanied by involuntary contractions of the _muscles_ of the outer third of the vagina, the ___uterus___, perineum, _rectum_, and the lower abdomen.

e. Recent research of Masters and Johnson has ___disprove___ the idea that there are two different kinds of ___orgasm___. There are no measurable _phycolgical_ differences between so-called ___vaginal___ and ___clitorus___ orgasms.

f. There is no ___counter pa___ in women to the male _refactor_ period.

Learning Objective 5

Describe some of the basic characteristics of initial sexual adjustments.

a. Many couples experience two types of sexual ___anxiety___: fear of _abnormality_ and fear of ___inadqacy___.

b. Recent studies show that ___married___ couples are having sexual ___intercourse___ more frequently than previously. For example, women questioned in ___1970___ reported a ___14___ percent higher frequency of intercourse than those questioned in ___1965___.

c. Increases in the frequency of intercourse are related to _education_ levels and to the use of _contraception_.

d. Wives between 26 and 30 years of age report having intercourse just under ___10___ times per ___month___. The frequency was still over ___4___ times per month for wives past the age of 50.

e. Two recent studies have shown that about ___56___ percent of all women report having orgasm ___always___ or ___almost___ always.

f. About ___2/3___ of married women report _satisfaction_ with their frequency of intercourse, but ___30___ percent state that intercourse occurs too _infrequatly_.

g. Many women indicate that too much ___emphasis___ has been placed on the female _orgasm_ and it appears to be true that there are many ___different___ forms of _good_ sexual adjustment in marriage.

106

Learning Objective 6

Describe the basic characteristics of extra-marital relationships.

a. Previously, there has been an assumption that _Cross sex_ friendships posed a great _threat_ to marriage. They were believed to carry a high _RISK_ of emotional and _Sexual_ involvement.

b. Today more women are _employed_ outside the home and more couples believe that not of all of any person's needs can be met by the _Spouse_ alone.

c. Some contend that people are capable of keeping their relationships _platoic_ while others suggest that _Sexual_ interest will arise as soon as _empathy_ is established.

d. The solution is for both friends to be _Aware_ of the nature of their relationship and to be completely honest about the _boundries_ of that relationship.

e. Three conditions that contribute to _Oxtramarital_ affairs are: _Lose_ of excitement in marriage, _needs_ that the spouse cannot fulfill, and _Sexual_ feelings for someone else.

f. One recent study of middle-class, middle-aged couples found that _68_ percent of the husbands and _28_ percent of the wives reported extra-marital sex. More recent findings suggest that women are _Catching_ up with the _men_ .

g. There is no _simple_ answer to the question of the effects of extra-marital affairs on _Marriage_.

h. Awareness of _oneself_ and one's _Relationships_ is probably the best protection against an extra-marital affair.

Learning Objective 7

Describe the basic characteristics of swinging.

a. Swingers believe that norms of sexual fidelity are _hypocritac_ and that all physical, sexual expression is _good_ .

b. Swinging sometimes occurs between _two_ couples who are _friends_ .

c. Couples who retire to bedrooms for _privacy_ are known as _closet_ swingers.

d. ___Coups___ are the preferred unit for __Recruitment__ into the swinging group.

e. There are four basic rules of swinging: disavowal of the double __Standard__, physical and __Impersonal__ sex, no pressure into accepting an __Unwanted__ sexual activity, and freedom to engage in many sexual activities without __disapproval__ of others.

f. There is no __evidence__ that swinging has either a positive or a negative effect on marital __stability__.

g. The principal reason reported for __dropping__ out of swinging was __jealousy__.

h. A recent study suggests that swinging is a __Male__ institution and not part of any sexual __Revolution__.

MULTIPLE CHOICE QUESTIONS

__A__ 1. The eighteen-inch tube which carries sperm to the seminal vesicles is the

    a. vas deferens.   c. glands.
    b. epididymis.   d. scrotum.

__B__ 2. The tube in which sperm are stored for maturation is the

    a. vas deferens.   c. glands.
    b. epididymis.   d. scrotum.

__D__ 3. The loose pouch of skin below the base of the penis is the

    a. vas deferens.   c. glands.
    b. epididymis.   d. scrotum.

__A__ 4. The folds enclosed within the labia majora are called the

    a. labia minora.   c. mons veneris.
    b. vulva.   d. cervix.

__B__ 5. The female external genitalia are called the

    a. labia minora.   c. mons veneris.
    b. vulva.   d. cervix.

__D__ 6. The lower end of the uterus is called the

    a. labia minora.   c. mons veneris.
    b. vulva.   d. cervix.

_C_ 7. The area covered with hair and fatty tissue over the pubic bone is called

    a. labia minora.   c. mons veneris.
    b. vulva.   d. cervix.

_A_ 8. Compared to 1965, rates of intercourse for women in 1970 had

    a. increased.
    b. decreased.
    c. increased for younger women but decreased for older women.
    d. increased for older women but decreased for younger women.

_A_ 9. Which of the following is not one of the stages of the sexual response?

    a. stimulation   c. plateau
    b. excitement   d. orgasm

_A_ 10. Increases in the frequency of marital intercourse are related to

    a. higher education and increased use of contraception.
    b. higher education and decreased use of contraception.
    c. lower education and increased use of contraception.
    d. lower education and decreased use of contraception.

_C_ 11. According to a 1972 study, _____ percent of all married women report having orgasm always or most of the time.

    a. 39   c. 59
    b. 49   d. 69

_C_ 12. In the same 1972 survey, _____ percent of the women reported that intercourse was too infrequent.

    a. 10   c. 30
    b. 20   d. 40

_C_ 13. Which of the following is not listed as a reason for the occurrence of extra-marital affairs?

    a. loss of excitement in marital sex
    b. needs the partner cannot fill
    c. needs for status
    d. strong sexual feelings for another

___D___ 14. A recent study of middle-class, middle-aged couples found that
_____ percent of the husbands and _____ percent of the
wives reported at least one extra-marital sexual relationship.

    a. 48, 18   c. 48, 28
    b. 68, 18   d. 68, 28

___b___ 15. Which of the following was <u>not</u> a classification reported in a recent study
of married women and their involvement in extra-marital affairs.

    a. traditional women   c. modern women
    b. liberated women   d. experimenting women

___D___ 16. The rules of swinging include

    a. an obvious double standard.
    b. pressure to accept all offers of sex.
    c. disapproval of oral, anal, or homosexual activities.
    d. a requirement of no emotional involvement.

___C___ 17. The reason most often reported for dropping out of swinging was

    a. loss of interest in sex.
    b. high levels of emotional involvement.
    c. jealousy.
    d. guilt.

___A___ 18. With respect to couples' involvement in swinging, the decision to participate was most often made by

    a. the husband.   c. the couple jointly.
    b. the wife.   d. the in-laws.

TRUE FALSE QUESTIONS

___F___ 1. F Frequent orgasm during menstruation tends to intensify menstrual cramping.

___F___ 2. F In a normal, healthy man, the supply of sperm is completely replaced in
about three to four hours after ejaculation.

___F___ 3. F The external female genitalia are called the vagina.

___F___ 4. F When women masturbate, they most often stimulate the clitoris directly.

___T___ 5. T The second phase of sexual arousal is called the plateau stage.

110

_F_ 6. The resolution stage in women also includes the refractory period.

_T_ 7. Recent research has disproved the idea that there are two kinds of orgasm.

_T_ 8. Wives with higher education report greater frequency of intercourse than less-educated wives.

_F_ 9. About 10 percent of married women stated that intercourse occurred too infrequently.

_T_ 10. One of the basic rules of swinging prohibits emotional involvement between sexual partners.

_F_ 11. Feelings of guilt are the reasons most often reported for dropping out of swinging.

_T_ 12. Most recent research findings indicate that swinging is basically a male-dominated practice.

MATCHING

_G_ 1. epididymis   a. external female genitalia

_B_ 2. prostate gland   b. provides seminal fluid

_I_ 3. sex during menstruation   c. first stage of arousal

_A_ 4. vulva   d. sex anxieties

_H_ 5. clitoris   e. last stage of arousal

_C_ 6. excitement   f. couples' sexual activities with others

_E_ 7. resolution   g. stores sperm

_D_ 8. abnormality and inadequacy   h. site of sexual arousal

_A_ 9. swinging   i. alleviates cramping

ESSAY QUESTIONS

1. Much recent public information indicates that married couples can obtain satisfaction from an overwhelming variety of different sexual patterns. If this is so, explain why so many couples continue to be preoccupied by fears about abnormality and inadequacy in their sexual behaviors and desires.

2. Explain why married couples of all ages are now having intercourse more fre-
    quently than ever before. What kinds of social conditions would be most likely
    to sustain or reverse this trend toward more frequent intercourse?

3. From your previous readings on the sexual conditioning of males and females,
    describe what swinging would be like if it were a female-dominated practice.

ANSWERS

Learning Objective 1

a. six, erection, size, sexual
b. spongy, excitement, erection
c. impotence, psychological
d. testicles, scrotum
e. sex, sperm
f. epididymis, vas, vesicle
g. prostate, Cowper's, orgasm

Learning Objective 2

a. organs, internal
b. tubes, vagina
c. follicles, ovum
d. cervix
e. taboos, menstruation
f. upper, vagina, nerve
g. vulva, majora, minora,
h. clitoris, glans

Learning Objective 3

a. Johnson, plateau, resolution
b. zone, penis, perineum, scrotum
c. excitement, cerebral, reflex
d. few, plateau
e. stimulation, orgasm, contractions, heartbeat, blood
f. resolution, refractory, erection

Learning Objective 4

a. clitoris, men
b. excitement, nipples, minora, enlarge
c. plateau, clitoris, minora, orgasm, decrease
d. orgasm, muscles, uterus, rectum
e. disproved, orgasm, physiological, vaginal, clitoral
f. counterpart, refractory

Learning Objective 5

a. anxiety, abnormality, inadequacy
b. married, intercourse, 1970, 14, 1965
c. educational, contraception
d. 10, month, 4
e. 56, always, almost
f. two-thirds, satisfaction, 30, infrequently
g. emphasis, orgasm, different, good

Learning Objective 6

a. cross-sex, threat, risk, sexual
b. employed, spouse
c. platonic, sexual, empathy
d. aware, boundaries
e. extramarital, loss, needs, sexual
f. 68, 28, catching, men
g. simple, marriage
h. oneself, relationships

Learning Objective 7

a. hypocritical, good
b. two, friends
c. privacy, closet
d. couples, recruitment
e. standard, impersonal, unwanted, disapproval
f. evidence, stability
g. dropping, jealousy
h. male, revolution

MULTIPLE CHOICE QUESTIONS

1.	a		10.	a
2.	b		11.	c
3.	d		12.	c
4.	a		13.	c
5.	b		14.	d
6.	d		15.	b
7.	c		16.	d
8.	a		17.	c
9.	a		18.	a

114

TRUE FALSE QUESTIONS

1.	F		7.	T
2.	F		8.	T
3.	F		9.	F
4.	F		10.	T
5.	T		11.	F
6.	F		12.	T

MATCHING

1.	g		6.	c
2.	b		7.	e
3.	i		8.	d
4.	a		9.	f
5.	h			

Chapter 10

FINANCIAL ADJUSTMENT

KEY TERMS AND CONCEPTS

Financial Family Life Cycle: Stages in the life of a couple which are defined by different levels of expense and income.

Financial Values: Values related to feelings about who will work at what kind of job and how money will be saved or spent.

Money Management: Use of money, where to live, use of credit, life insurance, investments, and taxes.

Budgeting: A financial practice which establishes priorities and provides that outgo does not exceed income.

Housing Choice: Determined by space needs, geographic location, life style, and decisions to rent or buy.

Credit: All methods of payment in which cash is not immediately exchanged for purchase of goods or services.

Life Insurance: A form of protection for dependents, low interest borrowing, and saving.

Borrowing: Methods for obtaining money in return for payment of an interest rate.

Unsecured Loans: The borrower has no collateral.

Savings: Systematic accumulation of money for protection against emergencies and for purchase of large items.

Investments: Methods intended to increase capital through interest, dividends, and growth.

Growth: The extent to which the value of an investment equals or exceeds the growth of the economy.

Yield: The effective interest rate paid on an investment.

Safety: The probability of losing all or part of one's investment.

Favorable Tax Treatment: The state encourages investment by reduction of the tax rate.

LEARNING OBJECTIVES

Fill in the words required to complete each sentence.

Learning Objective 1

Describe the financial adjustments of families at different stages of the life cycle.

a. When the young husband begins work, his _INCome_ is quite low, and the _demaNDS_ on it are almost overwhelming.

b. If both the young husband and wife hold _Job's_, they often achieve a feeling of relative _AfluENcy_.

c. Many couples have limited _goAls_ for the _wife_ working after marriage.

d. The first _BAby_ signals the beginning of 20 or more years of large and generally increasing _expeNses_.

e. A major insurance company estimates that it takes about _three_ times the father's _ANNUAl_ salary to support a child to the age of 18.

f. Today, fewer _OlD_ couples have to move in with their _childrew_.

g. The _INVeSTMeNT_ possibilities for the _PoST-PARET_ years are endless.

Learning Objective 2

Describe basic relationships between money and marital happiness.

a. Early studies of marital _hAppiewess_ and income yielded inconclusive or _NegaTive_ findings.

b. One view is that higher incomes are signs of one's _WORTh_ and also a _MRANS_ of purchasing more of the goods and _SeRuices_ that bring satisfaction.

c. A recent census study reported that ____72%____ percent of the ___household___ heads earning less than 5,000 dollars per year and ____83____ percent of the heads earning more than 15,000 dollars per year were in their first ___Marriage___ .

d. If money does not buy __MARITAL__ happiness, it does appear to serve as a ___deterrent___ to divorce.

e. Another recent study shows that people with over 15,000 dollars in annual income are more than ___twice___ as likely than people in the under-_3,000_ category to report being "very happy."

f. Up to some __minimum__ point, the __Adolescent__ size of one's income is probably an important ___factor___ in both happiness and financial adjustment.

Learning Objective 3

Describe how marital adjustment is affected by a couple's financial values.

a. People's values relate directly to what they want out of ___Life___ and how they achieve their __goals__ .

b. One basic financial concern is whether the ___wife___ should hold paid __employment__ .

c. Our __CORPRATE__ system often forces couples to make choices between one partner's __CAREER__ and the other's.

d. Up to _500,000_ employees are __transvered__ by their companies each year.

e. Additional corporate pressures dictate that the couple live somewhat better than the husband's immediate __Subordinates__ but not so well as his __Superiors__ .

f. Another source of conflict in corporate marriages is the husband's lavish living at the __COMPANYS__ expense, while the wife is forced to live rather __frugally__ .

g. Finally, one spouse may view __SAVINGS__ as a means of insuring __security__ , while the second spouse wants to enjoy the fruits of the couple's __income__ .

Learning Objective 4

Describe the basic principles of money management.

a. The best starting point in developing a workable __budget__ is to estimate one's annual __INCOME__ .

b. A general budget must be _translated_ into a plan for _Spending_ over each month or pay period.

c. Many different budgeting patterns will work as long as the couple plans the spending and _savings_, and as long as they _agree_ on how it is done.

d. As a couple's income grows, the proportion spent for food _decreases_, but the proportion spent for taxes _increases_.

e. Regardless of income level, the proportion spent for _housing_ tends to remain _constant_.

f. The cost of _monthly_ housing rental should be no more than one- _week's_ take-home pay.

g. In buying a house, the most common rule is that _total_ cost should not exceed two and one-half times one's total _annual_ income.

h. In _1974_, an amendment to the federal Capital Consumer Credit Protection Act prohibited credit _discrimination_ the basis of either _sex_ or marital status.

i. Listing the pros and cons of renting compared to buying a house involves _oversimplification_ in at least two respects: different life styles attract different _personality_ types, and a couple's needs over the life-cycle are _variable_.

Learning Objective 5

Describe the principal uses of credit in modern marriage.

a. In the United States, there are over _300_ million retail credit cards, _133_ million gasoline credit cards, and _93_ million bank credit cards in circulation.

b. One simple rule of credit limitation states that total _debt_ should not exceed _20_ percent of annual _take home_ income.

c. Interest on charge accounts not paid within the prescribed billing _period_ typically accrues at a rate of _18_ percent a year.

d. Banks encourage spreading credit-card payments over a period of months because of the high _interest_ rates that are charged on _unpaid_ balances.

e. _durable_ consumer goods are most often purchased with _Istallment_ credit.

f. The three preferred sources for borrowing money are life _INSURANCE_, commercial _BANKS_, and credit _UNIONS_. Those who cannot borrow from these sources frequently obtain _Secured_ loans from consumer _FINANCE_ companies.

Learning Objective 6

Describe the basic types of life insurance.

a. Most people begin to think about _Buying_ life insurance around the time they _MARRY_.

b. Ideally, life insurance should be adequate to cover the deceased partner's _debts_, _BURIAL_ expenses, and to provide _income_ support for the _Surviving_ spouse.

c. _term_ insurance affords more protection per _PREMIUM_ dollar than any other kind of policy.

d. Term insurance is purely for _protection_, and there is no _SAVINGS_ involved.

e. A useful variant on _Regular_ term insurance is the _decreasing_ term policy.

f. The two principal advantages of straight life insurance are that premium payments remain _Constant_, and that such policies accumulate a cash _value_.

g. _Endowment_ policies emphasize _SAVINGS_ more than protection.

h. Per _dollar_ of protection, endowment policies are the most _expensive_ form of insurance.

Learning Objective 7

Describe the basic principles of investment and tax planning.

a. Investment differs from saving in being oriented toward capital _growth_ rather than simply capital _Accumulation_.

b. In investment, three factors should be considered: _growth_, yield, and _Risk_.

c. _growth_ refers to the extent to which the value of the investment exceeds the expansion of the _economy_.

120

d. ___yeild___ refers to the effective interest ___RAte___ paid on the assets.

e. Investment ___INcome___ is given favorable treatment under the federal ___Income___ tax ___law___.

f. For investors who reach the highest tax ___brakets___, tax-free ___Municibal___ bonds are a valuable investment.

g. Employees without qualified retirement plans may establish ___Individual___ Retirement ___Acounts___, and self-employed persons may set up a ___Keogh___ Plan.

MULTIPLE CHOICE QUESTIONS

_A_ 1. Many college couples are able to accept comparative poverty because

   a. most of their friends are in similar circumstances.
   b. they have been raised in poverty.
   c. their religious beliefs approve of poverty.
   d. they enjoy criticizing the more materialistic culture of the everyday world.

_A_ 2. Compared to lower-income families, higher-income families show

   a. somewhat greater marital stability.
   b. about equal marital stability.
   c. somewhat lower marital stability.
   d. considerably lower marital stability.

_d_ 3. In general, the best place to begin developing a workable budget is with

   a. weekly income.   c. quarterly income.
   b. monthly income.   d. annual income.

_C_ 4. Credit-card interest charges typically amount to _____ percent per year.

   a. eight   c. eighteen
   b. thirteen   d. twenty-three

_d_ 5. Communal living arrangements typically encounter financial problems because

   a. everyone works at the same job.
   b. the use of food stamps creates legal problems.
   c. members invariably bicker over the spending of surplus money.
   d. the financial base is inadequate for this life style.

_b_ 6. The policies commonly available from an employer are examples of
_____ insurance.

    a. limited payment   c. decreasing term
    b. term   d. straight life

_d_ 7. A policy which requires payment of a fixed payment through the life of
the insured is an example of _____ insurance.

    a. limited payment   c. decreasing term
    b. term   d. straight life

_C_ 8. A policy in which protection ultimately decreases to zero is an example of
_____ insurance.

    a. limited payment   c. decreasing term
    b. term   d. straight life

_C_ 9. Which of the following is not one of the major criteria for evaluating
an investment opportunity?

    a. yield   c. value
    b. safety   d. growth

_B_ 10. A life insurance company estimates that it takes about _____ times
the father's annual salary to provide for a child to the age of 18.

    a. two   c. four
    b. three   d. six

_A_ 11. Compared to those with annual incomes under three thousand dollars, people
with incomes over 15,000 dollars were _____ times as likely to
report being "very happy."

    a. two   c. four
    b. three   d. five

_C_ 12. As a couple's income grows, the proportion of family income spent for
housing usually

    a. increases substantially.   c. remains constant.
    b. increases.   d. decreases.

_D_ 13. As a couple's income grows, the proportion of family income spent on food
typically

    a. increases substantially.   c. remains constant.
    b. increases.   d. decreases.

C 14.   About _____ of all new car purchases are made on credit.

    a. one-quarter   c. two-thirds
    b. one-half   d. four-fifths

b 15.   Which of the following is the most expensive source for obtaining personal loans?

    a. credit unions
    b. consumer finance companies
    c. commercial banks
    d. life insurance

A 16.   Which of the following types of life insurance requires payment of steadily increasing premium rates?

    a. term   c. straight life
    b. declining term   d. whole life

TRUE FALSE QUESTIONS

T 1.   Many college couples find it easy to accept their relative poverty because most of their friends are in a similar situation.

F 2.   Recent life insurance company estimates suggest that it takes the equivalent of one year of a father's annual salary to rear a child to age 18.

F 3.   Most recent research findings indicate that marital stability decreases as family income increases.

T 4.   Annual income is generally the best beginning figure for developing a workable family budget.

T 5.   Compared to those who rent, couples who purchase their own homes receive substantial tax benefits.

F 6.   Yield, growth, and safety are the three most important criteria for evaluating a life insurance policy.

T 7.   A recent survey of nineteen countries showed that high-income people were more likely than low-income people to report being "very happy."

F 8.   As family income grows, the proportion spent for food tends to increase.

F 9.   Consumer finance companies tend to be the cheapest sources of personal loans.

___T___10. Premium rates for term insurance increase with the age of the insured.

___T___11. Straight life insurance policies require the payment of a fixed premium throughout the insured's life.

___F___12. Municipal bonds are among the best investment opportunities for couples in lower income tax brackets.

MATCHING

___h___ 1. marital stability

___f___ 2. childrearing costs

___b___ 3. corporate marriage

___j___ 4. food

___A___ 5. housing

___C___ 6. taxes

___i___ 7. term insurance

___d___ 8. straight life insurance

___g___ 9. municipal bonds

___e___ 10. Keogh Plan

a. requires constant proportion of increasing income

b. frequent relocation

c. requires larger proportion of increasing income

d. fixed premium

e. retirement for self-employed

f. three times father's annual salary

g. exempt from federal tax

h. directly related to family income

i. only for protection

j. requires smaller proportion of increasing income

ESSAY QUESTIONS

1. Describe the financial planning characteristic of corporate marriage and explain how economic circumstances contribute directly and indirectly to the marital satisfaction of each partner.

2. Explain why costs of food, housing, and taxes require changing proportions of income for couples at different income levels.

3. Explain why investment and tax planning is most often handled by the husband, and describe specific steps that a couple might take to have the wife more involved in this type of financial planning.

124

ANSWERS

Learning Objective 1

a. income, demands
b. jobs, affluence
c. goals, wife
d. baby, expenses
e. three, annual
f. old, children
g. investment, post-parental

Learning Objective 2

a. happiness, negative
b. worth, means, services
c. 72, household, 83, marriage
d. marital, deterrent
e. twice, $3,000
f. minimum, absolute, factor

Learning Objective 3

a. life, goals
b. wife, employment
c. corporate, career
d. 500,000, transferred
e. subordinates, superiors
f. company's, frugally
g. savings, security, income

Learning Objective 4

a. budget, income
b. translated, spending
c. saving, agree
d. decreases, increases
e. housing, constant
f. monthly, week's
g. total, annual
h. 1974, discrimination, sex
i. oversimplification, personality, variable

Learning Objective 5

a. 300, 133, 93
b. debt, 20, take-home
c. period, 18
d. interest, unpaid
e. durable, installment
f. insurance, banks, unions, secured, finance

Learning Objective 6

a. buying, marry
b. debts, burial, income, surviving
c. term, premium
d. protection, savings
e. regular, decreasing
f. constant, value
g. endowment, savings
h. dollar, expensive

Learning Objective 7

a. growth, accumulation
b. growth, risk
c. growth, economy
d. yield, rate
e. income, income, law
f. brackets, municipal
g. Individual, Accounts, Keogh

MULTIPLE CHOICE QUESTIONS

1.	a	9.	c
2.	a	10.	b
3.	d	11.	a
4.	c	12.	c
5.	d	13.	d
6.	b	14.	c
7.	d	15.	b
8.	c	16.	a

TRUE FALSE QUESTIONS

1.	T	7.	T
2.	F	8.	F
3.	F	9.	F
4.	T	10.	T
5.	T	11.	T
6.	F	12.	F

MATCHING

1.	h	6.	c
2.	f	7.	i
3.	b	8.	d
4.	j	9.	g
5.	a	10.	e

Chapter 11

FAMILY PLANNING

KEY TERMS AND CONCEPTS

Low U.S. Fertility Rates: Birth rates have been dropping since 1957 and have now fallen well below the replacement level.

Childbearing Expectations: The number of children people say they want or expect to have.

National Organization for Non-Parents (NON): A group devoted to promoting childless life styles for married couples.

Contraceptive Techniques: Methods that permit intercourse with reduced risk of pregnancy.

The Pill: An oral contraceptive which most effectively reduces the risk of pregnancy.

The IUD (Intrauterine Device): A small metal, plastic, or nylon object inserted into the neck of the uterus for contraceptive purposes.

The Condom: A thin latex sheath that fits snugly over the erect penis.

Rhythm: A birth control method dependent upon estimating ovulation accurately.

The Diaphragm: A circular rubber device that blocks the entrance to the cervix.

Spermicidal Jellies, Creams, and Foams: Chemicals inserted into the vagina that immobilize sperm.

Withdrawal: A method of withdrawing the penis just prior to ejaculation.

Sterilization: A permanent and irreversible method for preventing pregnancy.

128

<u>Salpingectomy:</u> A surgical procedure which removes a section of each Fallopian tube.

<u>Laparoscopy:</u> Insertion of a laparoscope to burn out sections of the Fallopian tubes.

<u>Vasectomy:</u> Tying or cauterizing the vas deferens, the tubes which carry sperm from the testicles to the urethra.

<u>Counseling for Sterilization:</u> Necessary because of the irreversibility of the procedure.

<u>Abortion:</u> Surgical procedure for ending an unwanted pregnancy.

<u>Infertility:</u> Failure to attain conception. Drugs used to overcome infertility often cause multiple births.

LEARNING OBJECTIVES

Fill in the words required to complete each sentence.

Learning Objective 1

Describe the demographic background of fertility in the United States.

a. For the last twenty-five years, the U.S. birth ___RATE___ has been ___declins___ irregularly.

b. In ___1972___, the American fertility rate dropped below the ___Replacement___ level. The replacement level is presently calculated at ___2.1___ children per ___Couple___.

c. From 1967 to 1976, the ___Advaase___ number of children expected by married American women dropped from 3.1 to ___2.4___.

d. Women with high ___CAReeR___ commitments now appear to want ___fewer___ children.

e. Marital satisfaction appears to be greatest when the couple ___aghees___ on the number of children ___desired___.

f. Children are often a source of deep ___SAtifACTiou___ in many marriages, but they also interfere with ___MAniTAl___ adjustment.

Learning Objective 2

Describe the basic characteristics of childless marriages.

a. Only about _____5_____ percent of married couples remain *vouluthaly* child-less. Until recently, these couples were often defined as _*deviant*_.

b. Partners in _*Sunvins*_ childless marriages report the greatest __*Marital*__ happiness.

c. Childless husbands and wives view marriage as less _*Restnictive*_, and as present-ing fewer _*pnoblem*_.

d. Most voluntarily childless couples move through four stages: _*definet*_ period of postponement, indefinite period of postponement, emphasis of positive _*Advantases*_, and _*innevecible*_ decision not to have children.

e. In the same study, all the __*wives*__ reported being somewhat *stigmatized*

f. Overall, childless wives seem to be _*Satisfied*_ with their own situations, but they are under some __*phessunee*__ from a generally disapproving _*society*_.

g. In a recent Kansas study, wives who did not want children were about _____3_____ times as likely to hold _*professional*_ jobs.

h. A new organization dedicated to childlessness is called the _*National*_ Organ-ization for _*NOPAnantes*_

Learning Objective 3

Describe the principal birth control methods of modern contraceptive technology.

a. By the 1970s, the most popular birth control methods were the _*pill*_ and the _*intehlube*_ device.

b. Oral contraceptives were first marketed in ___*1960*___, and today about _____*10*_____ million American women currently use the Pill.

c. The most serious ___*side*___ effect of the Pill is an increased tendency to develop blood _*clots*_.

d. About _____*20*_____ percent of all women who begin the Pill discontinue its use within a year.

e. The _*IUD*_ device is now the second most popular *CONTRecepT* in America.

130

f. The third most widely used form of contraception among _Married_ couples is
    the _Condum_.

g. The _Rythm_ method is the only form of contraception that is not
    forbidden by the Roman Catholic Church.

h. Before the introduction of the _Pill_ and the Intrauterine Device, the
    diaphram was the most widely recommended contraceptive.

i. The remaining forms of birth control products are _Spermacides_, the douche,
    and _withdraul_.

Learning Objective 4

Describe the basic characteristics of sterilization for men and women.

a. Given high _divonce_ rates and the possibility of early _widoowhood_,
    the _irreversability_ of sterilization becomes an important consideration.

b. The _traditional_ technique of female sterilization is called the _Salpistomy_.

c. Because the salpingectomy is major _Sun Suny_, it is usually performed in
    conjunction with other _adominal_ operations.

d. A more recent and _simple_ technique of female sterilization is called
    Lapanoscopy.

e. Today, the total number of sterilizations performed on American men and women
    exceeds more than _One_ million per year.

f. The _Surgical_ sterilization of the male is called _Vasectomy_.

g. Following vasectomy, the male often develops _Antibodies_ that destroy unused
    Sperm.

h. Sterilization is now the most popular contraceptive among couples who have been
    Married for _10_ years or more.

i. Because sterilization is largely _Irreversible_, physicians are reluctant to
    perform these operations without _Counseling_ of the married couple.

Learning Objective 5

Describe recent abortion practices in the United States.

a. Until recently, most _States_ permitted abortion only when the
    Mothers life was endangered.

b. In the late ___1960's___ , several states passed ___Liberized___ abortion laws.

c. In January, ___1993___ , the United States Supreme Court ruled that abortion during the first ___13___ weeks of pregnancy is solely the decision of the woman and her ___physican___ .

d. More than ___⅕___ of all pregnancies in the United States are currently ___terminated___ by abortion.

e. For a full-term pregnancy, the death rate is almost ___9___ times higher than for first ___trimester___ abortion.

f. A group that calls itself ___Right___ to Life has been a strong opponent of ___Legalized___ abortion.

g. In 1976, the Supreme Court ruled that women are entitled to abortions without the consent of their ___husband___ or ___parents___ .

Learning Objective 6

Describe recent developments for helping infertile couples.

a. As many as 10 to ___15___ percent of all couples in the United States are plagued with ___infertility___ problems.

b. Most frequently, male ___infertility___ ranges from high to low, and artificial ___insemenation___ requires implanting the husband's ___semen___ in the wife's ___uterus___ .

c. Many physicians believe that ___emotional___ factors, such as ___tension___ , contribute to many fertility problems.

d. Greatest recent progress has occurred with the development of new ___fertility___ drugs.

e. The largest problem with fertility ___drugs___ is their tendency to produce ___multiple___ births.

f. Another side effect of fertility drugs is the ___development___ of ovarian ___cysts___ .

MULTIPLE CHOICE QUESTIONS

_C_ 1. Compared to marriages with children,

    a. childless marriages appear to be happier.
    b. childless marriages appear to be less happy.
    c. surviving childless marriages appear to be happier.
    d. surviving childless marriages appear to be less happy.

_C_ 2. The majority of voluntarily childless couples appear to

    a. have been pressured by family and friends to forego children.
    b. have deeply regretted not having children.
    c. have drifted into childlessness through a series of postponements.
    d. be people with personality characteristics unsuited to parenthood.

_d_ 3. The National Organization for Non-Parents

    a. restricts memberships to non-parents.
    b. includes about 6 million American members.
    c. idealizes parenthood as an experience suited only to the gifted few.
    d. argues that all fertility decisions should be carefully thought out.

_b_ 4. United States birth rates have been decreasing irregularly since

    a. 1952.   c. 1962.
    b. 1957.   d. 1967.

_b_ 5. Since 1972, the United States

    a. fertility rate has been above the replacement level.
    b. fertility rate has been below the replacement level.
    c. has attained zero population growth.
    d. has attained less than zero population growth.

_b_ 6. From 1967 to 1976 the average number of expected children has decreased from 3.1 to _____ per couple.

    a. 2.8   c. 2.0
    b. 2.4   d. 1.6

_d_ 7. Compared to couples who plan children, the wives of couples who plan no children are more likely to

    a. report serious health problems.
    b. be of higher I.Q.
    c. be of lower I.Q.
    d. hold professional jobs.

_d_ 8. The second most popular contraceptive in America is the

    a. Pill.   c. condom.
    b. diaphragm.   d. IUD.

_A_ 9. The traditional medical procedure for female sterilization is the

    a. salpingectomy.   c. lobotomy.
    b. vasectomy.   d. laparoscopy.

_D_ 10. The most recently developed procedure for female sterilization is the

    a. salpingectomy.   c. lobotomy.
    b. vasectomy.   d. laparoscopy.

_B_ 11. The surgical technique for male sterilization is the

    a. salpingectomy.   c. lobotomy.
    b. vasectomy.   d. laparoscopy.

_A_ 12. In 1973, the Supreme Court ruled that the decision to have a first trimester abortion must be left entirely to the woman and her

    a. physician.   c. lawyer.
    b. husband.   d. religious counselor.

_C_ 13. In 1976, approximately _____ abortions were performed in the United States.

    a. two hundred thousand   c. one million
    b. five hundred thousand   d. two and one-half million

_C_ 14. The death rate from a full-term pregnancy is about _____ times higher than the mortality rate for a first-trimester abortion.

    a. two   c. nine
    b. four   d. twenty

_b_ 15. Which of the following has <u>not</u> been opposed to legalized abortion?

    a. a majority of state legislatures
    b. National Organization for Women
    c. the Right-to-Life Movement
    d. the Roman Catholic Church

_b_ 16. Compared to babies conceived through conventional methods, babies conceived through artificial insemination are

    a. more likely to have birth defects.
    b. less likely to have birth defects.
    c. more likely to have higher I.Q. scores.
    d. less likely to have higher I.Q. scores.

_C_ 17. Which of the following is a principal side effect of fertility drugs?

    a. yeast infection
    b. internal hemmorhage
    c. multiple births
    d. spontaneous abortion

_C_ 18. In 1976, the Supreme Court ruled that a married woman could legally obtain an abortion

    a. in the second trimester of pregnancy.
    b. in the third trimester of pregnancy.
    c. without her husband's consent.
    d. only with her husband's consent.

TRUE FALSE QUESTIONS

_T_ 1. The replacement rate for the United States population is 2.1 children per family.

_F_ 2. Couples with larger families report more happiness than couples with smaller families.

_T_ 3. Surviving childless marriages tend to be more happy than marriages with children.

_T_ 4. Wives who do not want children are more likely to hold professional jobs.

_F_ 5. The National Organization for Non-Parents excludes couples with children as members.

_T_ 6. The pill is presently the most widely used contraceptive technique in the United States.

_T_ 7. The safest birth control procedure is the condom or diaphragm, backed up by a first-trimester abortion.

_F_ 8. Recent research by Masters and Johnson shows the diaphragm to be a more effective contraceptive than it was previously thought to be.

_T_ 9. The traditional technique of female sterilization is the salpingectomy.

_T_ 10. A more recently developed technique of female sterilization is the laparoscopy.

_T_ 11. All present techniques of sterilization should be regarded as irreversible.

_F_ 12. Approximately four million abortions are performed in the United States each year.

MATCHING

_D_ 1. replacement level   a. highest marital satisfaction

_G_ 2. expected fertility   b. abortion legal

_h_ 3. professional jobs   c. cause multiple births

_A_ 4. surviving childless marriages d. 2.1 children per family

_i_ 5. laparoscopy   e. male sterilization

_e_ 6. vasectomy   f. reduces birth defects

_b_ 7. first trimester   g. 2.4 children per family

_C_ 8. fertility drugs   h. reduce women's fertility

_f_ 9. artificial insemination   i. female sterilization

ESSAY QUESTIONS

1. Explain why surviving childless marriages tend to be happier than marriages with children, and describe the attitude changes that have led to greater social acceptance of voluntary childlessness.

2. Describe the relationship between declining birth rates and the availability of more effective contraceptive and abortion technology. What other social and individual processes appear to have contributed to the baby bust?

3. Some demographers have predicted a new baby boom for the 1980s. What are the chances this will occur?

4. Explain why popular attitudes toward abortion have changed so drastically in the last twenty years.

ANSWERS

Learning Objective 1

a. rate, declining
b. 1972, replacement, 2.1, couple
c. average, 2.4
d. career, fewer
e. agrees, desired
f. satisfaction, marital

Learning Objective 2

a. five, voluntarily, deviant
b. surviving, marital
c. restrictive, problems
d. definite, advantages, irreversible
e. wives, stigmatized
f. satisfied, pressures, society
g. three, professional
h. National, Non-Parents

Learning Objective 3

a. pill, intrauterine
b. 1960, 10
c. side, clots
d. 20
e. intrauterine, contraceptive
f. married, condom
g. rhythm, forbidden
h. pill, diaphragm
i. spermacides, withdrawal

Learning Objective 4

a. divorce, widowhood, irreversibility
b. traditional, salpingectomy
c. surgery, abdominal
d. simple, laparoscopy
e. one
f. surgical, vasectomy
g. antibodies, sperm

h. married, 10
i. irreversible, counseling

Learning Objective 5

a. states, mother's
b. 1960s, liberalized
c. 1973, 13, physician
d. one-fifth, terminated
e. nine, trimester
f. Right, legalized
g. husbands, parents

Learning Objective 6

a. 15, infertility
b. infertility, insemination, semen, uterus
c. emotional, tension
d. fertility
e. drugs, multiple
f. development, cysts

MULTIPLE CHOICE QUESTIONS

1. c
2. c
3. d
4. b
5. b
6. b
7. d
8. d
9. a

10. d
11. b
12. a
13. c
14. c
15. b
16. b
17. c
18. c

TRUE FALSE QUESTIONS

1. T
2. F
3. T
4. T
5. F
6. T

7. T
8. F
9. T
10. T
11. T
12. F

MATCHING

1. d
2. g
3. h
4. a
5. i

6. e
7. b
8. c
9. f

Chapter 12

HAVING CHILDREN

KEY TERMS AND CONCEPTS

Presumptive Signs of Pregnancy: Changes such as the absence of a period, "morning sickness," swollen breasts, frequent urination, and changes in the cervix.

Morning Sickness: A feeling of nausea at any time but particularly upon awakening.

Pregnancy Tests: Chemicals which, when mixed with urine, reveal an increase in the level of hormones.

First Trimester of Pregnancy: From conception to the end of the third month. Chances of miscarriage are the greatest.

Zygote: Fertilized ovum during the first two weeks.

Embryo: Fertilized ovum from the third to eighth week.

Fetus: Fertilized ovum from the ninth week until the end of the pregnancy.

Placenta: A spongy mass of blood vessels which carry nutrients to and waste products from the baby.

Amniotic Fluid: Fluid formed from some of the first cells of the developing fertilized ovum.

Second Trimester of Pregnancy: A sense of well being, fetal heartbeat, and "kicks" become more frequent.

Third Trimester of Pregnancy: The baby increases in size rapidly toward its average birth weight of 7½ pounds. Fatigue and sleep loss are common.

"Spotting:" A light menstrual-type bleeding that may signal a spontaneous abortion.

Rh Blood Type Complications: Possible mingling of the mother's blood and the baby's blood lead to the development of antibodies endangering the fetus.

Normal Presentation: The fetus' head faces downward so that it emerges first from the vagina.

Breech Presentation: The buttocks move into the cervix first.

Transverse Presentation: The fetus lies crosswise in the uterus.

Cesarean Section: A surgical procedure for delivery through the abdominal wall.

False Labor: Uterine contractions grow more pronounced late in the pregnancy but long before the onset of labor.

True Labor: Strong, regular, frequent contractions that gradually increase to 5 minutes apart, the appearance of a small plug of blood-stained mucous, and amniotic fluid.

The First Stage of Labor: From onset to the dilation of the cervix.

The Second Stage of Labor: From dilation of the cervix until actual birth, a period of approximately 20 minutes.

An Episiotomy: A small incision in the perineum to reduce the risk of torn tissue.

The Third Stage of Labor: Mucous is removed from the baby's mouth and throat; the physician cuts the umbilical cord, and the placenta is expelled.

"Natural Childbirth:" A term used to cover techniques which reduce medical intervention in childbirth. Fathers may also be included and may be present at birth.

"Rooming-In:" A newborn baby shares the mother's hospital room instead of residing in the nursery.

New Mother's Letdown: A post-partum sense of disappointment or sorrow during the first few weeks after birth.

New Father's Sense of Neglect: The new baby displaces the husband from the center of his wife's attention, and periods of sexual abstinence lead the new father to feelings of neglect.

Transition to Parenthood: The crisis of parenthood is negatively related to the level of marital adjustment.

Toddlerhood: Active crawling and the first faltering steps. Energy and curiosity are boundless and often carry the toddler into potentially dangerous situations.

Discipline: Teaching a child to avoid situations that endanger him physically or socially. The most common methods are distraction, reward, and punishment.

Preschoolers: A period during which the child emerges as a separate identity. A need to learn to distinguish between feelings and actions is most characteristic.

Parallel Play: Children playing side by side with little awareness of each other.

Parents as Persons: An attitude of couples who view parenthood as a source of personal growth rather than a burden.

LEARNING OBJECTIVES

Fill in the words required to complete each sentence.

Learning Objective 1

Describe the early signs of pregnancy.

a. The _____First_____ sign of pregnancy is typically a missed __Menstal__ period.

b. Other signs of pregnancy include "Morning _Sickness_," swollen _BREAST_, and increasing frequency of _Urination_.

c. There are two widely used pregnancy tests: one depends on _Micnasope_ examination and the second on _Chemical_ reaction.

d. Use of both tests provides a _Reliable_ result between 95 and __98%__ percent of the time.

e. Human pregnancy lasts for an _Avnage_ of __266__ days.

Learning Objective 2

Describe the first trimester of pregnancy.

a. The first trimester is the time from _Conception_ to the end of the _third_ month.

b. About ___1/5___ of pregnant women experience light ___Menstral Ty___ bleeding, called "___Spotting___."

c. No ___Restrictions___ are likely to be placed on the couple's ___Sexual___ activity.

d. The woman's ___RH___ blood ___Type___ is also checked in the first trimester.

e. For the first two weeks the ___fertalize___ ovum is called a ___Zygot___. For the next ___6___ weeks, it is an ___embryal___, and from then until birth it is called a ___fetus___.

f. Tiny blood vessels eventually become the ___placeta___, which is connected to the fetus by the ___Umbelical___ cord.

Learning Objective 3

Describe the second and third trimesters of pregnancy.

a. At about the middle of the ___fourth___ month, the physician can hear the fetal ___heartbeet___.

b. The baby also begins to "___kick___" as it grows larger and moves about in the ___uterus___.

c. Serious ___genetc___ problems in the fetus can be diagnosed with a procedure called ___Amiocentecs___

d. A by-product of amniocentesis is the ___detenmita___ of the ___sex___ of the baby.

e. If a serious ___defect___ is discovered in the fetus, the mother has the choice of a ___therepeutic___ abortion.

f. During the final ___trimester___, the fetus increases greatly in ___Size___.

g. Many physicians recommend that ___Intecones___ be discontinued approximately ___Six___ weeks before the baby is expected.

Learning Objective 4

Describe the principal stages of childbirth.

a. The baby ordinarily moves into a ___Normal___ position before ___birth___.

144

b. A breech presentation occurs when the _buttocks_ move into the _cirvex_ first.

c. A _trasveks_ presentation may require a _cesaren_ operation.

d. There are three signs of the onset of true labor: _regular_ and frequent contractions, the appearance of the "_show_," and the rupture of the _ammion_.

e. The first stage of labor lasts until the _dilation_ of the mother's _cenvir_.

f. The second stage of childbirth often requires the physician to make a small, surgical _incision_, called an _epitosny_.

g. Couples who prefer "_natural_ childbirth" object to what they consider to be excessive _medical_ interference with a natural, biological experience.

h. Many mothers report great _emotional_ satisfaction from more _crative_ participation in childbirth.

i. _rooming in_ facilities permit the mother to care for the baby in her own room.

Learning Objective 5

Describe the couple's basic adjustments to the new baby.

a. Elation over having the new baby at home is soon replaced by problems of _letdown_ and _neglect_.

b. During the first few weeks, the new _mother_ frequently experiences an emotional _letdown_.

c. The new father's needs and expectations no longer receive first _concern_ from his _wife_.

d. The father is also replaced somewhat in the mother's _affection_ and _attention_, and the father often experiences feelings of neglect and _resontment_.

e. The feelings of the father are often accompanied by a sense of sexual _diphatiov_, and intercourse is not usually resumed until _six_ weeks after the birth.

f. For parents, there is a _negative_ relationship between their _marital_ adjustment and the amount of _restment_ reported in the transition to parenthood.

g. Most couples report that their ___MANNAGES___ have ___Improved___ or remain un-changed since the baby's birth.

Learning Objective 6

Describe parental roles in the caring for young children.

a. Toddlers explore almost everything with insatiable ___Curi3ty___ and boundless ___energy___. Hence they require close and continuous ___Supervision___

b. A problem for many parents during toddlerhood is the protection of the ___home___ and its ___Contents___.

c. ___Restrictions___ that the child can understand are not likely to cause ___danger___.

d. Toddlerhood eventually merges into the ___preschool___ years.

e. Developing a firm sense of ___Identity___ is not easy for most ___children___.

f. Preschool children need special help in learning to distinguish between their ___feelings___ and their ___Actions___.

g. Couples who choose to be parents today are likely to have deep ___Emotional___ commitments to one another and be involved in long-range ___planning___.

h. The idea of parents as people means that the ___Rights___ and ___feeling___ of parents are as important as those of their children.

MULTIPLE CHOICE QUESTIONS

__b__ 1. The usual first sign of pregnancy is

   a. "morning sickness."
   b. a missed menstrual period.
   c. more frequent urination.
   d. swollen and sensitive breasts.

__C__ 2. Pregnancy tests involve chemical or microscopic analysis of the woman's

   a. blood.   c. urine.
   b. bile.   d. saliva.

C 3. Kits for testing pregnancy in the home cost about

    a. two dollars.   c. ten dollars.
    b. five dollars.   d. twenty-five dollars.

A 4. For more convenient analysis, pregnancy is divided into

    a. trimesters.   c. semesters.
    b. quarters.   d. fortnights.

A 5. Medical complications are most likely to occur if the mother's blood type
    is Rh-negative and the father's blood type is

    a. Rh-positive.   c. Rh-neutral.
    b. Rh-negative.   d. Rh-universal.

b 6. Which of the following is not one of the developmental stages of the
    fertilized ovum?

    a. fetus   c. embryo
    b. egg   d. zygote.

A 7. Which of the following is not one of the signs of the onset of true labor?

    a. pronounced restless in the fetus
    b. regular and frequent contractions
    c. appearance of the "show"
    d. rupture of the amnion

A 8. The first stage of childbirth lasts from the onset of labor until dilation
    of the

    a. cervix.   c. vagina.
    b. uterus.   d. hymen.

B 9. Which of the following is not one of the major fetal positions prior to
    birth?

    a. normal presentation   c. transverse presentation
    b. obverse presentation   d. breech presentation

d 10. The key event of the final stage of labor is the expulsion of the

    a. baby.   c. amnion.
    b. umbilical cord.   d. placenta.

b 11. A Cesarean section is most likely for the case of a fetus in a

a. normal presentation.   c. breech presentation.
b. transverse presentation.   d. obverse presentation.

b 12. Couples who object to excessive medical intrusion into childbirth frequently choose techniques associated with _____ childbirth.

a. painless   c. drugless
b. natural   d. artificial

b 13. Sexual intercourse is usually discontinued _____ weeks before the baby's birth and not resumed until _____ weeks after.

a. 3   c. 9
b. 6   d. 12

b 14. The extent of crisis precipitated by arrival of the new baby is

a. directly related to the couple's marital adjustment.
b. inversely related to the couple's marital adjustment.
c. unrelated to the couple's marital adjustment.
d. directly related to the father's feelings of sexual deprivation.

b 15. Over 85 percent of all couples report their marriages have _____ since the arrival of their baby.

a. either improved or worsened.
b. either improved or remained unchanged.
c. remained unchanged.
d. improved.

C 16. As many as _____ percent of the children born in the 1970s will spend part of their childhood in a one-parent family.

a. 20   c. 40
b. 30   d. 50

b 17. During the preschool period, it is most important that children learn to distinguish between their feelings and their

a. thoughts.   c. anger.
b. actions.   d. responsibilities.

C 18. When very young children are brought together, they most often engage in

a. cooperative play.   c. parallel play.
b. competitive play.   d. promiscuous play.

148

_b_ 19. The generation gap of the traditional family has been replaced to some
degree by the _____ gap of the modern family.

    a. personal   c. cultural
    (b.) communications   d. emotional

_b_ 20. Which of the following is <u>not</u> one of the major non-economic values of having
children?

    a. power   c. emotional security
    (b.) privilege   d. prestige

TRUE FALSE QUESTIONS

_T_ 1. The first sign of pregnancy is usually a missed menstrual period.

_F_ 2. "Spotting" during the first trimester usually implies that the pregnancy
was misdiagnosed.

_F_ 3. The risk with an Rh-negative mother's pregnancies decreases with each
further pregnancy.

_F_ 4. The second trimester of pregnancy usually brings more medical complications
than the first trimester.

_T_ 5. During the first two weeks of life, the fertilized ovum is called a zygote.

_T_ 6. A by-product of amniocentesis is the determination of the sex of the baby.

_T_ 7. A Cesarean section is most likely in the case of a transverse presentation.

_T_ 8. Rupture of the amnion is a sign of the onset of true labor.

_T_ 9. The final event of childbirth is the expulsion of the placenta.

_F_ 10. A majority of maternity hospitals now have rooming-in facilities.

_F_ 11. In a couple's initial adjustment to the baby, the father is likely to feel
an emotional letdown, while the mother feels neglected.

_F_ 12. The crisis precipitated by the arrival of the baby is unrelated to the
couple's level of marital adjustment.

MATCHING

f 1. pregnancy test f   a. birth of the baby

d 2. first trimester d   b. personal growth and development

h 3. second trimester h   c. inversely related to crisis

g 4. third trimester g   d. "spotting"

j 5. first stage of labor j   e. expulsion of the placenta

A 6. second stage of labor A   f. based on increased hormones

e 7. third stage of labor e   g. rapid increase in weight

C 8. marital adjustment c   h. amniocentesis

b 9. parents as people b   i. power, prestige, and competence

i 10. non-economic values i   j. dilation of the cervix

ESSAY QUESTIONS

1. Describe the basic research findings on the impact of childbirth on marital adjustment. Apart from the self-reports of the couples involved, in what other ways might we try to measure the impact of childbirth on marital adjustment?

2. Describe the emotional consequences most likely to ensue from the discontinuation of intercourse for six weeks before and after childbirth.

3. Describe the non-economic values couples realize by having children. Do the last twenty-five years of a steadily declining United States birth rate indicate that these non-economic values are losing their influence?

150

ANSWERS

Learning Objective 1

a. first, menstrual
b. sickness, breasts, urination
c. microscopic, chemical
d. reliable, 98
e. average, 266

Learning Objective 2

a. conception, third
b. one-fifth, menstrual-type, spotting
c. restrictions, sexual
d. Rh, type
e. fertilized, zygote, six, embryo, fetus
f. placenta, umbilical

Learning Objective 3

a. fourth, heartbeat
b. kick, uterus
c. genetic, amniocentesis
d. determination, sex
e. defect, therapeutic
f. trimester, size
g. intercourse, six

Learning Objective 4

a. normal, birth
b. buttocks, cervix
c. transverse, Cesarean
d. regular, show, amnion
e. dilation, cervix
f. incision, episiotomy
g. natural, medical
h. emotional, active
i. rooming-in

Learning Objective 5

a. letdown, neglect
b. mother, letdown
c. concern, wife
d. affection, attention, resentment
e. deprivation, six
f. negative, marital, crisis
g. marriages, improved

Learning Objective 6

a. curiosity, energy, supervision
b. home, contents
c. restrictions, damage
d. preschool
e. identity, children
f. feelings, actions
g. emotional, planning
h. rights, feelings

MULTIPLE CHOICE QUESTIONS

1.	b	11.	b
2.	c	12.	b
3.	c	13.	b
4.	a	14.	b
5.	a	15.	b
6.	b	16.	c
7.	a	17.	b
8.	a	18.	c
9.	b	19.	b
10.	d	20.	b

TRUE FALSE QUESTIONS

1.	T	7.	T
2.	F	8.	T
3.	F	9.	T
4.	F	10.	F
5.	T	11.	F
6.	T	12.	F

MATCHING

1. f	6. a
2. d	7. e
3. h	8. c
4. g	9. b
5. j	10. i

Chapter 13

DUAL CAREERS

KEY TERMS AND CONCEPTS

Dual-Career Marriage: The pursuit of careers with equal vigor and commitment of both husband and wife.

Family Planning of Dual-Career Marriages: Effective use of birth control resulting in fewer children by women with high work commitments.

The Dual-Career Decision: The decision of a woman to pursue her career indefinitely.

Geographic Mobility and Careers: A change of geographic location can often disrupt a spouse's career.

Competitiveness: Each spouse's career takes precedence over the demands of the partner's career.

Work Overload: Dual-career couples carry each of their careers plus family and domestic tasks.

Paid Household Help: Dual-career couples tend to use baby sitters, cleaning people, and live-in help.

Leisure Planning: Leisure must involve matching schedules for restoring the energies of both partners.

Entertainment Requirements: Dual-career couples tend to use commercial facilities to meet their professional and social obligations.

Kinship Ties: Continuing relationships with kin are difficult because the couple is geographically distant from interests and values that may have become quite different.

Dissolution of Dual-Career Marriages: Traditional expectations of the husband may conflict with equalitarian expectations of the wife.

154

LEARNING OBJECTIVES

Fill in the words required to complete each sentence.

Learning Objective 1

Compare traditional and dual-career marriages.

a. Young people today are more likely to believe in _equality_ between the sexes and in the right of women to full participation in the _occupational_ world.

b. Only __7__ percent of American families consist of a husband, a _nonworking_ wife, and __two__ children.

c. In a _dual career_ marriage, both partners pursue _individual_ careers with equal _commitment_

d. Research shows that women with high occupational _commitment_ use birth control more _successfully_

e. Dual-career marriages seldom have more than __two__ children.

f. More recent findings show no differences in the _marriage_ adjustment _scores_ of wives who choose to work and wives who choose not to.

Learning Objective 2

Describe the nature of dual-career marriages.

a. Most dual-career couples _marry_ relatively _late_.

b. The _decision_ to have dual careers is often made in _successive_ stages.

c. A new dual-career family faces the problem of finding _acceptable_ jobs in the same geographic _area_.

d. Families with working wives are more likely to move _within_ counties and less likely to move _between_ counties.

e. When dual-career couples make _long distance_ moves, there is some chance the _wife_ will drop out of the labor force _temporarily_.

f. A move by the husband tends to hinder the career opportunities of _working_ wives but increase the opportunities for _non-working_ wives.

Learning Objective 3

Discuss competitiveness, overwork, and division of labor in dual-career families.

a. Some career _Sacrafices_ are almost _Inevitable_ in dual-career marriages, however, disruptive _competition_ does not seem to occur.

b. A husband's _identication_ with his wife's career is a strong source of _solidanity_ in many marriages.

c. Other dual-career couples _Share_ their work to some extent, but where competition prevails there is a high probability of disruption of one of the _Careers_ or of the _Marages_ .

d. _employed_ mothers usually have less than _2/3_ the free time that their husbands enjoy.

e. To avoid impossible pressures, dual-career couples must change their _houskeeping_, childrearing, and _leisure_ patterns.

f. _traditional_ men appear to be in the _Minority_ in dual-career marriages.

g. Most dual-career partners report _Sharing_ most of their _household_ duties.

h. In all forms of dual-career adjustment, there are both _Satisfaction_ and _Costs_ .

Learning Objective 4

Discuss children's duties, domestic help, and leisure in dual-career families.

a. Children in dual-career families are likely to be taught _Resposiboity_ and cooperation from an early _Age_ .

b. Dual-career parents treat their children as _Contributing_ family members and take pride in their _Achiments_

c. Many families hire a second person in the home to perform the _tradition_ tasks of the _houswife_ .

d. A lower _quality_ of the household _environment_ may be one price for dual careers.

e. _Leisure_ in dual-career families must be _planned_ more carefully.

156

Learning Objective 5

Describe the social activities characteristic of dual-career families.

a. Dual-career couples __Avid__ lavish entertaining at __home__ .

b. When such couples are required to entertain __formaly__ , they are more likely
    to do it at __Restnuants__.

c. One partner often conducts __BUS'NESS__ entertainment without the other
    partner's _____ .

d. Dual-career couples more often draw their __Joint__ friends from the
    __wipes__ associates.

e. __Family__ ties play little or no role in the __decisions__ of dual-career
    families.

f. Except for __emotioal__ ties, dual-career couples have little in common with
    their __parents__ .

g. Continued kinship ties of the dual-career family are more likely to be based
    upon true __Affection__ and compatibility in basic __values__ .

Learning Objective 6

Describe the marital stability of dual-career couples.

a. Dual-career marriages are too __New__ for there to be much evidence about
    their __Stability__ .

b. One recent study shows there are __two__ major kinds of __problems__
    in dual-career marriages.

c. __dual careers__ wives reported seeking a more __egaltnian__ marriage pattern.
    Most of these divorces occurred by __Mutual__ agreement.

d. In other cases, both partners were so __Comitted__ to their careers they
    decided to give up on their __MARRIAGE__ .

e. Finally, some divorced women from dual-career marriages were able to obtain
    __Satisfation__ from a more __traditionl__ marriage.

MULTIPLE CHOICE QUESTIONS

_A_ 1. The numbers of dual-career marriages appear to be

    a. growing rapidly.   c. decreasing slightly.
    b. remaining constant.   d. decreasing rapidly.

_C_ 2. Compared to more traditional women, dual-career women

    a. have more children.
    b. have about the same number of children.
    c. have fewer children.
    d. use birth control less effectively.

_b_ 3. Lowest marital adjustment scores are reported by wives who

    a. choose to work.   c. choose to remain home.
    b. have to work.   d. have to remain home.

_A_ 4. Which of the following is <u>not</u> one of the three major stages of the woman's decision to work?

    a. before engagement   c. after marriage
    b. before marriage   d. after childbearing

_d_ 5. In decisions about where to live, priority is <u>least</u> likely to be given to the wife's career if

    a. the husband is self-employed.
    b. the husband is a professional.
    c. the wife works for a large organization.
    d. the husband works for a large organization.

_d_ 6. Compared to traditional families, dual-career families are

    a. more likely to move.
    b. less likely to move.
    c. more likely to move between counties, but less likely to move within counties.
    d. more likely to move within counties, but less likely to move between counties.

_d_ 7. A long-distance move by the husband usually increases the career opportunities for the wife who

    a. has several children.   c. is employed.
    b. has few children.   d. is unemployed.

_A_ 8. The most crucial factor in the success of a dual-career marriage is the

    a. husband's attitude.   c. children's attitude.
    b. wife's attitude.   d. parents' attitude.

_A_ 9. Compared to traditional husbands, dual-career husbands are

    a. more likely to help with household duties.
    b. equally likely to help with household duties.
    c. less likely to help with household duties.
    d. less likely to hire household help for their working wives.

_A_ 10. Compared to more traditional families, dual-career families plan

    a. longer and more frequent vacations.
    b. shorter and more frequent vacations.
    c. longer and less frequent vacations.
    d. shorter and less frequent vacations.

_C_ 11. The closest friends of most dual-career couples are likely to be

    a. traditional married couples.
    b. single people.
    c. other dual-career couples.
    d. divorced people.

_b_ 12. Dual-career couples tend to draw their friends

    a. from among the husband's colleagues.
    b. from among the wife's colleagues.
    c. equally from among the husband's and wife's colleagues.
    d. from couples who do not work for a living.

_C_ 13. Kinship ties for dual-career couples are more likely to be based upon

    a. financial advantage.
    b. feelings of family obligations.
    c. compatibility of values.
    d. needs to maintain appearances.

_d_ 14. Compared to more traditional couples, divorces among dual-career couples are

    a. more frequent.   c. more hostile.
    b. less frequent.   d. less hostile.

TRUE FALSE QUESTIONS

___T___ 1. The number of dual-career marriages is rapidly increasing.

___F___ 2. Wives who choose to work obtain lower marriage adjustment scores than wives who choose to remain home.

___F___ 3. Most dual-career couples marry earlier than traditional couples.

___T___ 4. The husband's attitude is one of the most important factors in the success of a dual-career marriage.

___F___ 5. Compared to traditional families, dual-career families are more likely to move between states.

___T___ 6. Dual-career marriages seldom have more than two children.

___F___ 7. Children in traditional families are given household responsibilities at an earlier age than children in dual-career families.

___T___ 8. Dual-career couples have longer and more frequent vacations than traditional couples.

___F___ 9. Dual-career couples are more likely to socialize with traditional couples than with other dual-career couples.

___T___ 10. Friendship choices of dual-career couples are more influenced by the wife's occupation than the husband's.

MATCHING

___g___ 1. family planning   g   a. occurs in three stages

___d___ 2. marital adjustment   D   b. longer and more frequent

___A___ 3. dual-career decision A   c. dual-career couples

___h___ 4. division of labor · h   d. lowest for wives who must work

___b___ 5. vacations b   e. divorce is less hostile

___C___ 6. friendship choice c   f. compatibility and basic values

___f___ 7. kinship relations f   g. more effective among the job committed

___e___ 8. marital disruption e   h. involves husband and children

ESSAY QUESTIONS

1. Explain why dual-career couples might be more likely than traditional couples to rear their sons and daughters in the same way.

2. Explain why the husband's attitude is more important than the wife's in making a dual-career marriage work.

3. Explain why divorce among dual-career couples may be less hostile and less disruptive than it is among more conventional couples.

ANSWERS

Learning Objective 1

a. equality, occupational
b. seven, non-working, two
c. dual-career, individual, commitment
d. commitment, successfully
e. two
f. marriage, scores

Learning Objective 2

a. marry, late
b. decision, successive
c. acceptable, area
d. within, between
e. long-distance, wife, temporarily
f. working, non-working

Learning Objective 3

a. sacrifices, inevitable, competition
b. identification, solidarity
c. share, careers, marriage
d. employed, two-thirds,
e. housekeeping, leisure
f. traditional, minority
g. sharing, household
h. satisfactions, costs

Learning Objective 4

a. responsibility, age
b. contributing, achievements
c. traditional, housewife
d. quality, environment
e. leisure, planned

Learning Objective 5

a. avoid, home
b. formally, restaurants
c. business,
d. joint, wife's
e. family, decisions
f. emotional, parents
g. affection, values

Learning Objective 6

a. new, stability
b. two, problems
c. dual-career, egalitarian, mutual
d. committed, marriage
e. satisfaction, traditional

MULTIPLE CHOICE QUESTIONS

1.	a	8.	a
2.	c	9.	a
3.	b	10.	a
4.	a	11.	c
5.	d	12.	b
6.	d	13.	c
7.	d	14.	d

TRUE FALSE QUESTIONS

1.	T	6.	T
2.	F	7.	F
3.	F	8.	T
4.	T	9.	F
5.	F	10.	T

MATCHING

1.	g	5.	b
2.	d	6.	c
3.	a	7.	f
4.	h	8.	e

Chapter 14

DIVORCE

KEY TERMS AND CONCEPTS

Divorce Rate: The number of divorces per 1,000 population.

Male Domination of Divorce: More divorces are sought by husbands than wives, but wives usually file for divorce.

Unhappy Marriages: Those in which partners described their marriage as unhappy, regretted their marriage, or had recently considered separation or divorce.

Divorce Laws in the United States: Each of the 50 states and the District of Columbia has its own unique divorce laws.

Traditional Divorce Philosophy: Grounds for divorce should be limited to a few serious offenses, divorce should be difficult to obtain and should establish guilt and innocence.

Adversary System: Each partner retains an attorney to gain the best settlement.

Plaintiff: The partner bringing suit and who claims to have been wrongfully treated.

Defendant: The person accused of misconduct.

No-Fault Divorce: Recognition that marriages should be ended when they are no longer workable.

Personal Experience of Divorce: Divorce carries an emotional impact that is similar to the grief cycle following death of a loved one.

Child Custody: Small children are more likely to be assigned to their mothers; the father is more likely to receive custody if the child is older, male, or expresses a preference.

Child Support: Obligation for financial support based on the father's ability to pay and the amount required to maintain the child.

<u>Post-Divorce Relationships</u>: Friendships linked with the former marriage frequently dwindle. Involvement with relatives increases while in-law involvement diminishes.

LEARNING OBJECTIVES

Fill in the words required to complete each sentence.

Learning Objective 1

Describe the background characteristics of divorce in contemporary America.

a. Both the _____ and rates of divorce have _____ over the last decade.

b. Divorce rates are highest among _____ people, those who marry _____, and the poor.

c. In the United States, about one marriage out of every _____ will end in divorce.

d. The probability of _____ is greatest during the _____ year of marriage.

e. The _____ of couples seeking divorce drops with each _____ of marriage.

f. About seventy-five percent of all divorce _____ are filed by the _____.

g. _____ are now becoming more _____ than ever before in ending unsatisfactory marriages.

h. Women are entering marriage today with new _____, and they are showing new _____ to end marriages that are unsatisfactory.

Learning Objective 2

Describe the principal causes of divorce.

a. Recent findings show that marital dissatisfaction is greatest among _____, blacks, and persons with _____ income.

b. Additional characteristics associated with marital dissatisfaction are poor _____ and _____ health and heavy _____.

c. A study of 600 divorce applications in Cleveland showed that the largest complaint of both _____ was _____ cruelty.

d. About 37 percent of wives and 3 percent of husbands also complained of _____ abuse.

e. The second most frequent complaint of both wives and husbands was _____ of home and _____.

f. Husbands are more likely than wives to complain of _____ incompatibility, sexual _____, and in-law problems.

Learning Objective 3

Describe the divorce laws of the United States.

a. The divorce laws of no _____ states are _____ alike.

b. People facing divorce today are finding themselves coping with both _____ and _____ philosophies.

c. _____ governments have traditionally looked upon divorce as a _____ evil.

d. Traditional divorce law pits each partner against the other in a legal _____ to determine who shall be judged _____.

e. The _____ system requires that all divorce proceedings have a _____ and a defendant. This rule sets the stage for transforming the _____ battle into a _____ one.

f. Often the wife's attorney advises a more generous _____ settlement than the _____ is offering, and the husband often learns that the divorce will cost more than he _____.

g. The adversary nature of the divorce process works against the partner's _____ and remaining on _____ terms afterwards.

Learning Objective 4

Describe the movement toward no-fault divorce.

a. In 1969, _____ became the first state to eliminate the _____ concept of divorce.

b. This law also provided for approximately _____ division of the couple's _____.

c. Over the following three years, the divorce _____ in California increased _____ than the national average.

d. By _____, all but three states had enacted some form of no-fault divorce _____.

e. No-fault divorce helps minimize the spouse's _____ that they are being _____.

f. In Florida, the _____ of no-fault divorce suits have been filed by _____.

g. The movement towards no-fault divorce appears to have wide _____ support and it suggests that divorce will be more common and more _____ in the future.

Learning Objective 5

Describe the personal experience of divorce.

a. The divorced person often feels _____ and that he or she has _____ in the marriage.

b. In addition, the divorcing person almost _____ suffers disapproval.

c. Divorce also introduces severe _____ to the person's _____.

d. In addition, there are no grieving _____ and little public _____ for the victims of divorce.

e. Eventually the _____ passes and the divorced person gradually comes to feel _____ again.

f. While divorce is an _____ experience, it is also a step towards emotional _____ and self-_____ for many people.

Learning Objective 6

Describe arrangements for child custody and support following divorce.

a. Most families do not have enough income to support two _____ without suffering a drop in their standard of _____.

b. Which parent receives _____ custody of the children is specified by the _____.

c. Most courts take the position that young children of both _____ need to be with their _____. However, with _____ boys, preference in custody is often given to the _____.

d. The law holds that the father is _____ for the _____ support of his children.

e. The spouses and their _____ may decide on the amount of child support, however, the amount must be ratified by the _____.

f. Many judges are likely to _____ the amount of child _____.

Learning Objective 7

Describe the relationship of divorced people to friends and their community.

a. Most people divorce not only a mate but also a set of _____ and almost an entire way of _____.

b. Few people are _____ for the lack of _____ they get from friends after the divorce.

c. Most _____ divorced people are _____. Their old friends may _____, or take sides, or don't know how to deal with the _____.

d. In about _____ of the cases, the divorced person experiences a closing of ranks with his or her _____.

e. Most divorced people report feeling no _____ toward their former spouse's _____.

f. For many people, the _____ suffering of divorce is preferable to perpetuating a _____ mistake.

g. Divorce is also a _____ experience and it is often a step toward a richer and more _____ life.

MULTIPLE CHOICE QUESTIONS

_____1. Which of the following variables is <u>not</u> associated with the divorce rate?

    a. political affiliation
    b. age at first marriage
    c. race
    d. income

_____2. More couples who are destined to become divorced separate during the _____ year of marriage.

    a. first   c. fifth
    b. second   d. seventh

_____3. In 1975, agencies that specialize in locating missing persons reported

    a. more runaway husbands than wives.
    b. more runaway wives than husbands.
    c. equal numbers of runaway husbands and wives.
    d. decreased numbers of runaway children.

_____4. Which of the following variables is <u>not</u> associated with marital dissatis-faction?

    a. poor mental health
    b. poor physical health
    c. heavy drinking
    d. heavy smoking

_____5. Which of the following is the most frequently cited complaint of divorcing wives?

    a. neglect of home and children
    b. mental cruelty
    c. physical abuse
    d. sexual incompatibility

_____6. Which of the following is the most frequently cited complaint of divorcing husbands?

    a. neglect of home and children
    b. mental cruelty
    c. physical abuse
    d. sexual incompatibility

_____7. Which of the following complaints is cited more often by the divorcing husband than by the wife?

    a. neglect of home and children
    b. mental cruelty
    c. physical abuse
    d. sexual incompatibility

_____8. The first state to introduce no-fault divorce was

    a. New York   c. California
    b. Michigan   d. Florida

_____9. Which of the following states is without a form of no-fault divorce legislation?

    a. Alabama   c. Texas
    b. Arkansas   d. Illinois

_____10. The majority of states have

    a. replaced traditional divorce with no-fault divorce.
    b. rejected no-fault divorce.
    c. added no-fault divorce to traditional divorce.
    d. rejected traditional divorce.

_____11. The major consequence of no-fault divorce in Florida was

    a. increased divorce rate.
    b. decreased divorce rate.
    c. more husbands filing for divorce.
    d. more wives filing for divorce.

_____12. About _____ percent of all divorced mothers never receive any child support from the fathers of their children.

    a. 20   c. 60
    b. 40   d. 80

_____13. Recent findings suggest that about _____ percent of divorced fathers obtain custody of their children.

    a. 2   c. 6
    b. 4   d. 15

_____14. About _____ percent of remarried women report a birth during a period of marital disruption.

   a. 5   c. 25
   b. 15   d. 45

_____15. Which of the following is <u>not</u> one of the reasons why traditional divorce courts have favored the mother in child custody awards?

   a. The mother more often requests custody of the children.
   b. Children need their mothers more than their fathers.
   c. Mothers are better at the parental role.
   d. The father must earn a living.

_____16. The father is more likely to be awarded custody if

   a. the child is younger.
   b. the child prefers to live with the mother.
   c. the child is a male.
   d. he threatens to default on child support payments.

_____17. The emotional impact of divorce is best compared to

   a. winning a contest.
   b. experiencing bereavement.
   c. getting lost in a forest and being found.
   d. having a baby.

_____18. The most important effect of divorce on friendship is

   a. to strengthen the friendship.
   b. similar to the effect of other major changes in life.
   c. to align friends on one side or the other.
   d. to decrease the probability of a divorced person making new friends.

TRUE FALSE QUESTIONS

_____1. The United States divorce rate has nearly doubled in the last ten-year period.

_____2. The divorce rate among white couples is higher than among black couples.

_____3. Agencies that specialize in locating missing persons now report more runaway husbands than runaway wives.

_____4. Heavy drinking is one of the major variables associated with marital dis-
satisfaction.

_____5. The most frequent complaint of divorcing husbands and wives is sexual incom-
patibility.

_____6. In 1975, Massachusetts became the first state to offer no-fault divorce.

_____7. There is evidence that no-fault divorce increases the number of petitions
filed by husbands.

_____8. About one-fourth of the remarried women in the United States report a birth
during a period of marital disruption.

_____9. Courts usually favor the mother in awarding custody of the children.

____10. The impact of divorce on friendship is different from the effect of most
other major life changes.

MATCHING

_____1. probability of divorce   a. most common divorce complaint

_____2. cause of unhappy marriage   b. pits partner against partner

_____3. mental cruelty   c. support of divorced spouse

_____4. divorce laws   d. change with life's circumstances

_____5. adversary system   e. no imputation of guilt

_____6. no-fault divorce   f. differ for each state

_____7. child support   g. higher for the young, poor, and black

_____8. alimony   h. more often awarded to mother

_____9. child custody   i. father's responsibility

____10. friendships   j. poor mental and physical health

ESSAY QUESTIONS

1. Explain why people often fail to give the same emotional support to the divorced that they give to friends and relatives who are passing through other life crises.

2. How can the statement that husbands more often want the divorce be reconciled with the finding that wives have many more specific complaints about their marriages?

3. To what extent is the grief cycle following divorce likely to be similar to the emotional trauma of widowhood?

ANSWERS

Learning Objective 1

a. numbers, rates
b. black, young
c. three
d. separation, first
e. proportion, year
f. petitions, wife
g. women, agressive
h. expectations, determination

Learning Objective 2

a. wives, low
b. physical, mental, drinking
c. sexes, mental
d. physical
e. neglect, children
f. sexual, infidelity

Learning Objective 3

a. two, exactly
b. traditional, no-fault
c. state, necessary
d. contest, guilty
e. adversary, plaintiff, marital, legal
f. property, husband, expects
g. cooperation, friendly

Learning Objective 4

a. California, adversary
b. equal, property
c. rate, less
d. 1977, legislation
e. feelings, victimized
f. majority, husbands
g. public, humane

Learning Objective 5

a. guilty, failed
b. inevitably
c. threats, self-esteem
d. rituals, support
e. trauma, whole
f. ego-shattering, maturity, fulfillment

Learning Objective 6

a. households, living
b. legal, court
c. sexes, mother, older, father
d. responsible, financial
e. lawyers, judge
f. raise, support

Learning Objective 7

a. friends, life
b. prepared, support
c. recently, lonely, disapprove, situation .
d. one-fifth, family
e. hostility, parents
f. temporary, marital
g. learning, meaningful

MULTIPLE CHOICE QUESTIONS

1.	a	10.	c
2.	a	11.	c
3.	b	12.	b
4.	d	13.	c
5.	b	14.	c
6.	b	15.	a
7.	d	16.	c
8.	c	17.	b
9.	d	18.	b

TRUE FALSE QUESTIONS

1.	T	6.	F
2.	F	7.	T
3.	F	8.	T
4.	T	9.	T
5.	F	10.	F

MATCHING

1.	g	6.	e
2.	j	7.	i
3.	a	8.	c
4.	f	9.	h
5.	b	10.	d

Chapter 15

PARENTS WITHOUT PARTNERS

KEY TERMS AND CONCEPTS

Infant Responses to Divorce: Babies respond to the feelings of anxiety, anger, or sorrow of those caring for them.

Preschooler Responses to Divorce: Emotional dependence on two parents may lead a child to feelings of guilt and fear that past misconduct has led to the disappearance of one parent.

School-Age Children's Responses to Divorce: Aware of parental problems, these children need an honest, reassuring explanation and the reestablishment of stable lives as quickly as possible.

Adolescent Reactions to Divorce: Most teenagers achieve a measure of objectivity toward their parents' problems.

Setting Limits: The parent without a partner is tested by the children to find out what sorts of behavior will be tolerated in the absence of the second parent.

Household Responsibility: The single parent must delegate tasks to the children, who acquire a sense of responsibility.

Sharing of Confidences: The parent must resist making the children into confidants.

Provision of Role Models: Arrangements that allow the children to share in the absent parent's daily life.

Parents Without Partners: A national organization with local chapters that provide information, companionship, and social activities.

Resumption of Dating: May create some awkwardness because earlier dating behaviors feel inappropriate, but companionship provides much needed support.

Sexual Reinvolvement: Deprived of sexual activity, it is almost inevitable that divorced men and women will become sexually active within a short time.

Coed Post-Divorce Living: An emerging pattern of sharing one's household with a member of the opposite sex as a method of reducing expenses and workload.

LEARNING OBJECTIVES

Fill in the words required to complete each sentence.

Learning Objective 1

Describe the impact of one-parent families on younger children.

a. About _____ percent of parents without partners are _____.

b. Most often _____ families are created by _____. Over _____ million children live in one-parent families.

c. Feelings of great anxiety, anger, or sorrow in the _____ may produce general symptoms of upset in the _____. However, as soon as the parent's emotional _____ is passed, the baby's normal _____ resumes.

d. The emotional upset of the _____ is likely to be more apparent and _____ than that of the infant.

e. The preschooler should have the _____ to visit with the absent _____ frequently.

Learning Objective 2

Describe the impact of one-parent families on older children.

a. Older children usually _____ something of what is happening to their _____.

b. The explanation for the separation should come from the parents _____, but the most important thing is that the explanation be _____.

c. School-aged children are also likely to take _____ in the conflict between their _____.

d. The most helpful outcome for school-aged children is for the _____ to reorganize their _____ as efficiently and calmly as possible.

e. Most teenagers acquire a degree of _____ about their parents' divorce and try to _____ what has happened.

f. Teenagers eventually get their own hold on _____, and learn to deal with their now _____ parents both as parents and as _____.

Learning Objective 3

Describe the life styles of mothers without partners.

a. Sooner or later the divorced _____ has to get a _____ .

b. Getting a job typically has two effects on the divorced woman: it bolsters her _____ , and raises her _____ of living.

c. The mother who is _____ of a household is likely to become more capable and more self-assured in the world of _____ and _____ .

d. Mothers without partners face challenges in at least four areas of childrearing: _____ limits, giving _____ , sharing _____ , and providing role _____ .

e. When the mother sets reasonable but _____ limits on her children's behavior, everyone settles down again to a _____ pattern of living.

f. Most divorced mothers manage to cope with household demands by _____ the responsibility with their _____ .

g. It is difficult for divorced mothers to know how much of their own inner _____ and _____ to share with their children.

h. Children who see their parents coping well with their own _____ statuses are likely to grow up prepared to assume their _____ as adult men and women.

Learning Objective 4

Describe the social life of the divorced mother.

a. The local chapters of _____ Without Partners emphasize the exchange of _____ and ideas and the development of understanding, help, and _____ .

b. Most chapters also have _____ programs and they frequently become the divorced mother's connection with the larger _____ .

c. _____ for the divorced mother may begin _____ before the divorce is granted.

d. There is often a certain _____ and hesitancy about the divorced mother's early efforts at _____ .

e. Most divorced women eventually _____ and motherhood without a

_____ is usually only a temporary phase.

f. A pervasive sexism tends to emphasize the sexual _____ of men, while _____ those of women.

g. About _____ of all divorced women eventually begin to have sexual _____ again.

h. For many divorced men and women there is likely to be a period of fairly casual _____ with _____.

i. Overall, divorced women reported great _____ with their _____ relationships.

Learning Objective 5

Describe the life of the single-parent father.

a. A recent Minneapolis study showed that child _____ was awarded to the father in _____ percent of the contested cases.

b. Many women today feel less _____ to seek _____ than they used to.

c. Fathers without partners are less likely than mothers to experience a great _____ in their _____ of living.

d. When a father has custody, both parents may have to do more to prevent the _____ from feeling their _____ has deserted them.

e. Friends, acquaintances, and relatives are likely to have a more difficult time _____ a father custody _____ than a mother custody one.

f. The experiences of males have not emphasized the _____ of nutritious meals, _____, and the care and repair of _____.

g. Divorced fathers probably press their _____ into the sharing of _____ tasks more than divorced mothers do.

h. In the cases of both divorced mothers and fathers there will be _____ shocks, _____, and the need to build new adult _____.

Learning Objective 6

Describe the development of coed living among divorced men and women.

a. One alternative for parents without partners is to find another person to help

_____ the _____ of living.

b. A recently emerging pattern of living involves a woman with _____, and
    a _____ man who shares their dwelling and some of their _____.

c. Many divorced women see no _____ issue in sharing their homes with
    a _____.

d. There is usually an agreement on _____ of labor and each person is free
    to continue his or her _____ life.

e. People who enter into these coed living arrangements are likely to be seeking
    the _____ and comfort of a fairly _____ family _____.

f. One minor _____ of these living arrangements frequently arises for
    _____.

g. The single man typically leaves the shared dwelling to pursue his _____
    activities on the _____.

h. For some _____ people, coed living is probably the route to
    _____.

MULTIPLE CHOICE QUESTIONS

_____1. For the divorced mother, having to get a job

        a. lowers her self-esteem.
        b. provides a status superior to that of divorced housewife.
        c. lowers her standard of living because the ex-husband stops alimony
            payments.
        d. decreases her network of social contacts.

_____2. Compared to divorced parents without child custody, divorced parents with
          custody of their children are likely to remarry

        a. more slowly.
        b. after about the same length of time.
        c. somewhat more quickly.
        d. considerably more quickly.

_____3. About _____ percent of the heads of one-parent families are women.

        a. 65   c. 85
        b. 75   d. 95

_____4. Which of the following are most likely to see their divorced parents as people?

    a. infants   c. school-aged children
    b. preschoolers   d. adolescents

_____5. Which of the following sense that their emotional security is dependent on both parents?

    a. infants   c. school-aged children
    b. preschoolers   d. adolescents

_____6. Which of the following need an honest explanation of the parents' divorce?

    a. infants   c. school-aged children
    b. preschoolers   d. adolescents

_____7. Which of the following is <u>not</u> one of the major areas in which divorced mothers face challenges in childrearing?

    a. providing role models   c. setting limits
    b. giving responsibility   d. sharing financial responsibilities

_____8. A national organization that is devoted to helping divorced parents escape social isolation is

    a. Parents Alone.   c. Parents Without Partners.
    b. Parents Anonymous.   d. Promiscuous Parents.

_____9. Recent data suggest that about _____ percent of divorced women have had sexual intercourse since their divorce.

    a. 52   c. 72
    b. 62   d. 82

_____10. The same study showed that about _____ percent of the divorced women who had post-marital intercourse confined it to only one man.

    a. 2   c. 22
    b. 12   d. 32

_____11. Compared to when they were married, divorced women were

    a. considerably less likely to reach sexual climax.
    b. somewhat less likely to reach sexual climax.
    c. equally likely to reach sexual climax.
    d. more likely to reach sexual climax.

_____12. A recent Minnesota study showed that child custody was awarded to the father in _____ percent of the contested cases.

a. 8   c. 28
b. 18   d. 38

_____13. Compared to mothers without partners, fathers without partners are

a. more likely to experience a drop in their standard of living.
b. less likely to experience a drop in their standard of living.
c. more likely to resume dating immediately following the divorce.
d. less likely to resume dating immediately following the divorce.

_____14. Of divorced men, the _____ father stands out as being happiest with his situation.

a. full-custody   c. quarter-time
b. half-time   d. less-than-quarter-time

_____15. The _____ father is the most eager to remarry.

a. full-custody   c. quarter time
b. half-time   d. less-than-quarter-time

_____16. The _____ father is <u>least</u> likely to be involved with a new woman.

a. full-custody   c. quarter-time
b. half-time   d. less-than-quarter-time

_____17. The _____ father considers the role of provider to be paramount.

a. full-custody   c. quarter-time
b. half-time   d. less-than-quarter-time

_____18. The coed living arrangement most frequently involves

a. a divorced woman and a divorced man.
b. a divorced woman and a single man.
c. a single woman and a divorced man.
d. a single woman and a single man.

TRUE FALSE QUESTIONS

_____1. About 85 percent of all parents without partners are men.

_____2. Over 17 million children live in one-parent families.

_____3. Infants frequently respond to their parents' divorce.

_____4. Preschool children frequently acquire a degree of objectivity about their parents' divorce.

_____5. Divorced women are likely to look first to their ex-husbands to help solve their financial problems.

_____6. Sharing confidences is one of the areas of childrearing in which the divorced mother faces new challenges.

_____7. At most meetings of Parents Without Partners, the divorced men outnumber the divorced women.

_____8. Divorced women are less likely to reach sexual climaxes than when they were previously married.

_____9. Fathers without partners usually face a larger drop in their standard of living than mothers without partners.

_____10. Compared to other fathers, the divorced half-time father stands out as being the happiest with his situation.

_____11. The coed living arrangement is most likely to involve a single woman and a divorced man with his children.

_____12. For many couples, coed living is a step to remarriage.

MATCHING

_____1. infants   a. acquire a degree of objectivity

_____2. preschoolers   b. 82 percent of divorced women

_____3. school-age children   c. helps the divorced escape isolation

_____4. adolescents   d. happiest with his situation

_____5. Parents Without Partners   e. emotionally dependent on both parents

_____6. sexual reinvolvement   f. divorced woman and single man

_____7. fathers without partners   g. least likely involvement with new woman

_____8. half-time father   h. don't know what is happening

_____9. full-time father   i. most anxious to remarry

_____10. quarter-time father   j. require an honest explanation

_____11. coed living   k. standard of living less likely to decline

ESSAY QUESTIONS

1. Describe dating and sexual reinvolvement for divorced fathers and explain how it differs from the case of divorced mothers.

2. Explain why friends, acquaintances, and relatives often find it more difficult to understand a father-custody divorce than a mother-custody divorce.

3. Describe the coed living arrangement presented in the text and speculate on the most likely outcomes of this arrangement as the relationship between the man and the woman develops.

ANSWERS

Learning Objective 1

a. 85, women
b. one-parent, divorce, seven
c. mother, infant, crisis, development
d. preschooler, pervasive
e. opportunity, parent

Learning Objective 2

a. understand, parents
b. jointly, honest
c. sides, parents
d. parents, lives
e. objectivity, understand
f. reality, separated, people

Learning Objective 3

a. mother, job
b. self-esteem, standard
c. head, work, money
d. setting, responsibility, confidences, models
e. firm, cooperation
f. sharing, children
g. feelings, needs
h. divorced, roles

Learning Objective 4

a. Parents, experiences, companionship
b. social, community
c. dating, effectively
d. awkwardness, dating
e. remarry, partner
f. frustrations, ignoring
g. four-fifths, intercourse
h. experimentation, sex
i. satisfaction, sexual

Learning Objective 5

a. custody, 38
b. pressure, custody
c. drop, standard
d. children, mother
e. understanding, divorce
f. preparation, housekeeping, clothing
g. children, household
h. financial, loneliness, friendships

Learning Objective 6

a. share, expenses
b. children, single, lives
c. moral, man
d. division, social
e. support, conventional, setting
f. complication, dating
g. dating, outside
h. divorced, remarriage

MULTIPLE CHOICE QUESTIONS

1.	b	10.	b
2.	a	11.	d
3.	c	12.	d
4.	d	13.	b
5.	b	14.	b
6.	c	15.	a
7.	d	16.	c
8.	c	17.	d
9.	d	18.	a

TRUE FALSE QUESTIONS

1.	F	7.	F
2.	F	8.	F
3.	T	9.	F
4.	F	10.	T
5.	T	11.	F
5.	T	12.	T

MATCHING

1. h
2. e
3. j
4. a
5. c
6. b

7. k
8. d
9. i
10. g
11. f

Chapter 16

REMARRIAGE

KEY TERMS AND CONCEPTS

Remarital Happiness: Recent evidence suggests 80 to 90 percent of remarriages are likely to be satisfying. Only a small percentage of those who divorce once will divorce again.

Reconstituted Families: Marriages involving at least one spouse with children who has remarried.

Family Integration: The more positive the relationship between sets of children from former marriages, the higher the level of integration of the family.

"Going Together" by the Formerly Married: Interaction tends to be straightforward, informal, and home centered. Emotional and physical intimacy are established very quickly.

Ex-Spouse Relationships: Complications arise when the former spouse has not completely given up emotional ties.

New Spouse and Ex-Spouse Relationships: The new and ex-spouse often have much in common.

Adjustment to Hostility of Outsiders: Family members, friends, and associates may feel hostile toward the remarriage.

Stepparenthood: Becoming a co-parent while recognizing the continuing involvement of the biological parent.

Assimilation of a Stepparent: Until enough time has passed for the family to have acquired shared experiences, the stepparent will tend to feel like an outsider.

LEARNING OBJECTIVES

Fill in the words required to complete each sentence.

Learning Objective 1

Describe the remarriage satisfaction of the divorced.

a. The _____ of divorced people living in continued loneliness and unhappiness is generally _____.

b. _____ of the divorced _____ within three years.

c. Of all people who have entered _____ marriages, fewer than 10 percent of the men and _____ percent of the women have been _____.

d. It is presently unknown whether divorce _____ from remarriages will be closer to those from remarriages in the _____ or to those from _____ marriages of the present.

e. In a recent Toronto study, over _____ percent of both husbands and wives reported that their marriages were "very _____." Only 5 to 10 percent of the couples rated their remarriages as "_____."

f. Marital happiness among the remarried must also take account of relationships between the _____ and their _____.

Learning Objective 2

Describe step-kin relationships among the remarried.

a. Scholars have traditionally emphasized the _____ aspects of _____ families.

b. Among a large sample of remarriages _____ percent of the adjustments were rated excellent, _____ percent were rated good, and _____ percent were rated poor.

c. Remarriage following _____ yields a higher proportion of excellent adjustments than does remarriage following _____.

d. The _____ men who married women with children made more excellent adjustments with their _____ than did men who were widowed or divorced.

e. A high percentage of poor adjustments occurs among _____ women who marry men with _____.

f. The _____ of life in families _____ through remarriage is relatively high.

Learning Objective 3

Describe family integration among the remarried.

a. A recent Cleveland study of reconstituted families showed that _____ percent were highly integrated, _____ percent were moderately integrated and _____ percent were judged to have low integration.

b. When parent-stepchild relationships are _____, most families are judged to be poorly _____.

c. The adjustment between each spouse and the other _____ children is critically important to the _____ of the entire family.

d. Compared to _____, younger children seem to get along better with their _____.

e. Relationships among _____ appear to be better in those families which have borne a new _____.

f. It is likely that better remarriages tend to produce additional _____, or that shared babies tend to increase everyone's _____ with the new family.

Learning Objective 4

Describe the courtship period that precedes remarriage.

a. Except for the very _____, those who are approaching remarriage tend to be rather direct and _____.

b. Both partners will tend to _____ interpersonal _____ somewhat cautiously.

c. In the dating of the divorced, _____ activities usually take precedence over formal or _____ activities.

d. It may only be weeks before the partners are sharing emotional and _____ intimacy in a _____ setting.

e. The confidences shared by the divorced person lead to reassurance and _____ from the other, or the _____ quickly withers.

f. Men and women approaching remarriage have been accustomed to sharing their _____ and they know the pleasures of _____.

g. Physical _____ increases the _____ that the man and woman feel for one another.

h. Finally, the couple's movement toward _____ will often depend on how the _____ respond to the relationship.

Learning Objective 5

Describe adjustments to outsiders by the remarried.

a. The _____ frequently enters the family in his or her role as a natural _____ of the children.

b. There are no _____ to state the kinds of relationships that are _____ and proper between ex-spouses.

c. _____ adjustments involving new spouses and ex-spouses are complex, varied, and often _____.

d. It is not _____ that the new spouse and the ex-spouse are often much _____.

e. In some cases, the new spouse and the ex-spouse become something like _____ and _____.

f. Responses of _____ and acquaintances to the new marriage depends on whether these people perceive some kind of triangle _____.

g. Some friends and associates take _____ in almost any _____. But others may make their _____ known only when the prospect of _____ develops.

h. New friends and co-workers are unlikely to be more than mildly _____ about the couple's former _____ lives, and they will probably treat the couple as a new _____.

Learning Objective 6

Describe the principal adjustments of stepparenthood.

a. The term stepparent came into use at a time when _____ generally followed the _____ of one of the natural parents.

b. There was little _____ of the possibility that _____ and affection might develop between the stepparent and the stepchild. Consequently, _____ developed of stepparents as harsh, cold, punitive, and

_____.

c. The two initial events with which the new stepparent must cope are the children's _____ ties to the biological parent and the _____ presence of that parent.

d. Children are more likely to respect and _____ a stepparent who encourages their closeness with their _____ parent.

e. Only after children have gained _____ will they develop _____ and love for their stepparent.

f. The _____ for the new stepparent is a _____ which confronts many children.

g. Two events that aid the integration of the stepparent into the new family are _____ and a new _____.

h. Adoption allows the stepparent to become the _____ parent, and to assume full _____ for the children.

i. When the remarried couple have _____ of their own, the _____ of the new family tends to be _____.

MULTIPLE CHOICE QUESTIONS

_____1. A Toronto study of the remarried showed that _____ percent of the couples considered their marriage to be unsatisfactory.

    a. 5-10   c. 20-30
    b. 10-20   d. 40-50

_____2. About 50 percent of those who remarry do so within about _____ years of their divorce.

    a. 2   c. 5
    b. 3   d. 7

_____3. An Ohio study of reconstituted families found that the groups with the best adjustments with their stepchildren were

    a. divorced fathers.   c. never-married fathers.
    b. divorced mothers.   d. never-married mothers.

_____4. Compared to singles, courtship among the formerly married tends to

    a. be more formal.
    b. be less involved with home-centered activities.
    c. move more quickly toward sexual intimacy.
    d. occur over a longer period of time.

_____5. The speed with which a couple moves towards remarriage depends on

    a. how quickly they become intimate.
    b. how their children respond to their relationship.
    c. their socio-economic status and education.
    d. their sexual compatibility.

_____6. Impressionistic evidence suggests that new spouses and ex-spouses are

    a. very much alike.
    b. very different from each other.
    c. unlikely to get along.
    d. unlikely to see much of each other.

_____7. Adoption is more probable when the natural parent is

    a. still single.   c. far away.
    b. the mother.   d. still contributing child support.

_____8. The groups with the lowest percentage of excellent adjustments with their stepchildren were

    a. divorced fathers.   c. never-married mothers.
    b. divorced mothers.   d. never-married fathers.

_____9. The quality of parent-stepchild relationships is most closely related to the family's overall

    a. cohesion.   c. cooperation.
    b. integration.   d. isolation.

_____10. Compared to teenaged children, younger children appear to

    a. get along better with their stepmothers.
    b. get along more poorly with their stepmothers.
    c. get along better with their stepfathers.
    d. get along more poorly with their stepfathers.

_____11. The term stepparent came into existence at a time when remarriage generally followed the _____ of one of the natural parents.

    a. divorce   c. death
    b. desertion   d. dismemberment

_____12. Which of the following is not one of the reasons given by child psychologists for problematic relationships between stepparents and stepchildren?

    a. reminder of the parent's sexual intercourse with the ex-spouse
    b. absence of a legal bond between stepparent and stepchild
    c. lack of any clear incest taboo between stepparent and stepchild
    d. excessive preparation of the stepparent for his or her new role

_____13. Adoption allows the stepparent to become the _____ parent.

    a. natural   c. legal
    b. symbolic   d. surrogate

_____14. Compared to those who remarry following widowhood, couples who remarry following divorce are more likely to report

    a. considerably more marital satisfaction.
    b. more marital satisfaction.
    c. equal marital satisfaction.
    d. less marital satisfaction.

_____15. The majority of remarried couples rate their marital adjustment as

    a. excellent.   c. good
    b. above average.   d. poor

_____16. The principal determinant of family integration scores following remarriage is

    a. the sexual compatibility of the remarried couple.
    b. the financial status of the remarried couple.
    c. the quality of the parent-stepchild relationship.
    d. the quality of the children's relationship with the ex-spouse.

TRUE FALSE QUESTIONS

_____1. Remarriage following widowhood is more likely to be successful than remarriage following divorce.

_____2. The majority of remarriages involving divorced couples eventually end in another divorce.

_____3. The best combination for a satisfactory remarriage is a single man who marries a divorced woman with children.

_____4. Compared to younger children, older children report getting along better with their stepmothers.

_____5. Courtship among the divorced involves sexual intimacy more quickly than courtship among the never-married.

_____6. How rapidly the partners move toward remarriage depends more on their financial status than on their children's behavior.

_____7. Impressionistic evidence suggests that the new spouse will be very similar to the ex-spouse.

_____8. Children are more likely to respect a stepparent who opposes their closeness with their natural parent.

_____9. Adoption allows the stepparent to become the natural parent.

_____10. When the remarried couple have children of their own, the solidarity of the new family tends to be weakened.

MATCHING

_____1. divorced people

_____2. single man-divorced mother

_____3. single woman-divorced father

_____4. family integration

_____5. sexual intimacy

_____6. spouse and ex-spouse

_____7. stepparent

_____8. adoption

_____9. new children

a. similar to each other

b. increase family solidarity

c. least marital satisfaction

d. stereotyped as harsh and unloving

e. legal parenthood

f. affected by parent-stepchild relationship

g. stereotyped as lonely and unhappy

h. occurs more quickly among the divorced

i. greatest marital satisfaction

ESSAY QUESTIONS

1. There is considerable evidence to suggest that becoming a successful stepmother is more difficult than becoming a successful stepfather. Explain why this appears to be the case.

2. Since natural parents and adoptive parents are extensively prepared for the roles they will assume, explain how prospective stepparents might also be more adequately prepared for their roles.

3. Since remarriage tends to be with someone who is quite similar to one's ex-spouse, what prevents the remarriage from eventually terminating in divorce?

ANSWERS

Learning Objective 1

a. stereotype, false
b. one-half, remarry
c. second, 15, redivorced
d. rates, past, first
e. 80, happy, unsatisfactory
f. parents, stepchildren

Learning Objective 2

a. problem, reconstituted
b. 64, 16, 16
c. widowhood, divorce
d. single, stepchildren
e. single, children
f. quality, created

Learning Objective 3

a. 45, 34, 21
b. poor, integrated
c. spouse's, welfare
d. teenagers, stepmothers
e. stepchildren, baby
f. children, identification

Learning Objective 4

a. young, straightforward
b. approach, intimacy
c. homecentered, commercial
d. physical, family-like
e. support, relationship
f. beds, sex
g. intimacy, closeness
h. remarriage, children

Learning Objective 5

a. ex-spouse, parent
b. guidelines, appropriate
c. long-term, surprising
d. surprising, alike
e. friends, confidants
f. friends, situation
g. sides, divorce, feelings, remarriage
h. curious, marital, family

Learning Objective 6

a. remarriage, death
b. recognition, love, stereotypes, unloving
c. emotional, physical
d. love, biological
e. reassurance, trust
f. name, dilemma
g. adoption, baby
h. legal, responsibility
i. children, solidarity, increased

MULTIPLE CHOICE QUESTIONS

1.	a	9.	b
2.	b	10.	a
3.	c	11.	c
4.	c	12.	d
5.	b	13.	c
6.	a	14.	d
7.	c	15.	a
8.	c	16.	c

TRUE FALSE QUESTIONS

1.	T	6.	F
2.	F	7.	T
3.	T	8.	F
4.	F	9.	F
5.	T	10.	F

MATCHING

1. g
2. i
3. c
4. f
5. h

6. a
7. d
8. e
9. b

Chapter 17

RETIREMENT

KEY TERMS AND CONCEPTS

Retirement: Withdrawal from a field of paid employment.

"Early" Retirement: Retirement prior to the date required by the worker's organization.

Arbitrary Retirement Age: Social Security and most pension plans set age 62 or 65 as the usual retirement date.

Financial Loss: When people stop working, their total income is almost always smaller.

Loss of Work Setting: The loss of a place to go interrupts physiological, social, and emotional rhythms and a period of adjustment is inevitable.

Social Contact Loss: A loss of daily interaction with work mates, and a loss of topics for thought and conversation.

Loss of Meaningful Tasks: The loss of a site that requires problems to be solved is likely to lead to a loss of one's abilities unless new challenges are found quickly.

Loss of a Reference Group: A loss of one's occupational reference group leaves a gap in one's identity.

Disengagement: Gradual withdrawal from work or any other significant activity.

Marital Happiness: Studies of retired people report that marriage is deeply satisfying and improves over time.

LEARNING OBJECTIVES

Fill in the words required to complete each sentence.

Learning Objective 1

Describe the role of retirement in the later family life cycle.

a. Retirement is the _____ of men and women from _____ employment.

b. If the working husband and the working wife are of about the same _____, they may retire _____.

c. About _____ million people in the United States have already reached retirement age, and the number has _____ rapidly.

d. Men who reach the age of 65 can now expect to live for an average of _____ more years, and women of 65 can expect to live almost _____ more years.

e. The _____ population has become _____ older. For example, since 1900 the _____ of the 85 age group has increased _____ times.

f. As a proportion of _____ earnings, retirement _____ decreases more for men than for women.

Learning Objective 2

Describe the personal factors in the couple's adjustment to retirement.

a. The most important problems that affect retired couples are losses of _____, of demand for _____, of social _____, of meaningful _____, and of a reference _____.

b. When the individual is not permitted to _____, he or she is denied a major source of _____.

c. Work not only provides _____ and self-esteem, but it is also a source of _____ social _____.

d. Only the development of a _____ new interest will _____ the retired person's abilities.

e. Loss of _____ with one's work group threatens one's _____ identity.

Learning Objective 3

Describe the procedures for planning retirement.

a. Ideally, people should be able to _____ gradually from _____.

b. Many _____ and self-employed people have _____ for phased withdrawal from their work.

c. The couple must acknowledge that _____ will come whether or not they _____ for it.

d. Retirement and _____ may help to cause _____.

e. However, disengagement from work can also be followed by _____ with _____.

f. Increasingly, people over age 65 are becoming a social _____ as well as a _____ category. Many of the retired are also banding together for _____ action.

Learning Objective 4

Describe the reorganization of domestic schedules that follows retirement.

a. Too much "_____" is as hard on a _____ as too little.

b. When the couple are suddenly together 24 hours a day, adjustments in the _____ may be as _____ as occupational adjustments.

c. Domestic adjustment to retirement is often more troublesome for _____ couples than those in which the _____ worked outside the _____.

d. Couples who have been together for decades seldom _____ after _____.

e. The adjustment to reorganized schedules is sometimes _____, but most couples manage it in a reasonably short _____.

Learning Objective 5

Describe the impact of retirement on marital happiness.

a. Many people do not _____ much about marital happiness in retirement, or they assume that it is not _____.

b. Approximately _____ percent of retired people rate their marriages as
    very happy or _____ .

c. More than half of the retired people reported that their marriages were happier
    at _____ than at any other _____ .

d. Marriages appear to be major sources of _____ for most people who are
    confronting the infirmities and reduced _____ of old age.

e. Six _____ conducted between 1963 and 1973 showed greater happiness and
    enjoyment of life among women at the _____ stage.

Learning Objective 6

Describe living arrangements and family cohesion among the retired.

a. During early retirement, about _____ of the women and _____ of
    the men have already been widowed.

b. Couples may be classified as high or low _____ types and as having close-
    knit or loose-knit _____ networks. The resulting four types help us to
    understand the functioning of _____ marriages and to predict the impact
    of widowhood on the _____ .

c. The last years of couples in a high-cohesion, close-knit _____ are
    likely to be fulfilling and _____ . _____ to widowhood occurs
    within a relatively short time.

d. For couples in a high-cohesion, loose-knit network, the _____ of widow-
    hood must be suffered _____ . Often a spiral of deterioration in
    _____ , emotional, and _____ health begins to occur in the
    survivor at this time.

e. In the low-cohesion, close-knit network, the _____ of widowhood passes
    quickly because the most important _____ in the survivor's life are
    still _____ .

f. In the low-cohesion, loose-knit network, the _____ has little to look
    forward to other than _____ .

MULTIPLE CHOICE QUESTIONS

_____1. At present, about _____ million in the United States have already
          reached retirement age.

a. 13   c. 23
b. 18   d. 28

_____2. Among people over the age of 65, about _____ percent own their own
         homes.

         a. 55   c. 75
         b. 65   d. 85

_____3. In a recent study of older husbands and wives, the largest percentage of
         couples complained about

         a. their marriages.
         b. unsatisfactory housing.
         c. crime in the streets.
         d. the rate of inflation.

_____4. Which of the following is <u>not</u> listed as one of the major problems to con-
         front the retired?

         a. loss of finances
         b. loss of social contacts
         c. loss of sexual prowess
         d. loss of a reference group

_____5. The co-workers who provide the individual with a sense of identification
         are an example of

         a. social group   c. reference group
         b. political group   d. compliance group

_____6. The occupational group with the best opportunity for gradual disengagement
         from work consists of

         a. factory workers   c. civil servants
         b. business executives   d. self-employed professionals

_____7. About _____ percent of retired people rate their marriages as
         happy or very happy.

         a. 64   c. 84
         b. 74   d. 94

_____8. The same study showed that the majority of marriages among the retired
         had

         a. improved.   c. deteriorated.
         b. remained about the same.   d. terminated in divorce.

_____9. When retired people were asked about the major problems of their present lives, they most frequently mentioned

    a. poor health.   c. unsatisfactory housing.
    b. insufficient money.   d. their marriages.

_____10. When retired people were asked about the major problems of their present lives, they least often mentioned

    a. poor health.   c. unsatisfactory housing.
    b. insufficient money.   d. their marriages.

_____11. When the couple is not particularly close and has several meaningful relationships with others, the result is the

    a. high family cohesion, close-knit network.
    b. high family cohesion, loose-knit network.
    c. low family cohesion, close-knit network.
    d. low family cohesion, loose-knit network.

_____12. When the couple virtually lives for each other and has little involvement with others, the result is the

    a. high family cohesion, close-knit network.
    b. high family cohesion, loose-knit network.
    c. low family cohesion, close-knit network.
    d. low family cohesion, loose-knit network.

_____13. When the couple is not close and does not have meaningful relationships with others, the result is the

    a. high family cohesion, close-knit network.
    b. high family cohesion, loose-knit network.
    c. low family cohesion, close-knit network.
    d. low family cohesion, loose-knit network.

_____14. When the couple is emotionally close and has meaningful relationships with others, the result is the

    a. high family cohesion, close-knit network.
    b. high family cohesion, loose-knit network.
    c. low family cohesion, close-knit network.
    d. low family cohesion, loose-knit network.

_____15. The poorest adjustments to widowhood are likely to occur in

    a. high cohesion families.   c. close-knit networks.
    b. low cohesion families.   d. loose-knit networks.

_____16. In which of the following combinations is life likely to have little
         meaning even before widowhood?

    a. high family cohesion, close-knit networks
    b. high family cohesion, loose-knit networks
    c. low family cohesion, close-knit networks
    d. low family cohesion, loose-knit networks

TRUE FALSE QUESTIONS

_____1. There are presently about 43 million retired people in the United States.

_____2. Women who reach the age of 65 can expect to live for an average of another
        17 years.

_____3. Since 1900, the number of people in the United States population over 84
        years of age has increased 17 times.

_____4. Retirement incomes are about $7,000 per year lower per couple than pre-
        retirement incomes.

_____5. Loss of sexual prowess is one of the most important factors in the personal
        adjustment of the retired.

_____6. The process of leaving one's work over a period of time is called gradual
        dismemberment.

_____7. Many of the retired are now banding together for political action.

_____8. Retirement is also likely to bring the happiness of the couple's finally
        being together without the interruption of regular work.

_____9. In a survey of retired people, unsatisfactory housing was the most fre-
        quently mentioned problem.

_____10. Several surveys have shown that women at the post-parental stage are
         happier than those who still have children at home.

_____11. Adjustment to widowhood is easier for couples in loose-knit rather than
         close-knit networks.

_____12. Life is likely to have least meaning for couples in low-family cohesion,
         loose-knit networks.

MATCHING

_____ 1. retirement

_____ 2. life expectancy

_____ 3. 85 age group

_____ 4. home ownership

_____ 5. reference group

_____ 6. gradual disengagement

_____ 7. reorganization of schedules

_____ 8. close-knit network

_____ 9. loose-knit network

_____ 10. unsatisfactory housing

a. increased 17 times since 1900

b. source of identification

c. more problematic for traditional couples

d. better adjustment to widowhood

e. 13-17 years after age 75

f. slow withdrawal from employment

g. frequent complaint of the retired

h. withdrawal from paid employment

i. poor adjustment to widowhood

j. three-quarters of retired couples

ESSAY QUESTIONS

1. Explain why a majority of retirement-age couples report increased marital satisfaction.

2. Most of this chapter is focused on the husband's withdrawal from paid employment. Are the problems of the retiring wife likely to be similar or different from those of the retiring husband?

3. Explain why organized groups of retired people have managed to greatly increase the political power of the aged in the last two decades.

208

ANSWERS

Learning Objective 1

a. withdrawal, paid
b. age, together
c. 23, increased
d. 13, 17
e. elderly, increasingly, size, 17
f. preretirement, income

Learning Objective 2

a. finances, skills, contacts, tasks, group
b. work, identity
c. income, meaningful, relationships
d. consuming, challenge
e. identification, personal

Learning Objective 3

a. disengage, work
b. professional, opportunities
c. retirement, plan
d. disengagement, aging
e. reengagement, life
f. group, population, political

Learning Objective 4

a. togetherness, marriage
b. home, troublesome
c. traditional, wife, home
d. divorce, retirement
e. traumatic, time

Learning Objective 5

a. think, important
b. 94, happy
c. retirement, period
d. satisfaction, resources

e. surveys, postparental

Learning Objective 6

a. one-half, one-fifth
b. cohesion, social, aging, survivors
c. networks, rewarding, adjustment
d. grief, alone, social, physical
e. trauma, relationships, intact
f. survivor, death

MULTIPLE CHOICE QUESTIONS

1. c
2. c
3. b
4. c
5. c
6. d
7. d
8. a

9. c
10. d
11. c
12. b
13. d
14. a
15. d
16. d

TRUE FALSE QUESTIONS

1. F
2. T
3. T
4. T
5. F
6. F

7. T
8. F
9. T
10. T
11. F
12. T

MATCHING

1. h
2. e
3. a
4. j
5. b

6. f
7. c
8. d
9. i
10. g

Chapter 18

WIDOWHOOD

KEY TERMS AND CONCEPTS

Profile of Widowhood: Almost 50% of the women and 20% of the men over 65 have lost their mates. There are four times as many widows as widowers.

Reintegration Value of the Caretaker Role: A lifetime of responsibility for domestic tasks provides the widow with a channel for working off the physical effects of grief.

Chances for Remarriage: Being outnumbered four to one, the widower has a greater pool of potential mates, and his remarriage is often viewed more favorably.

Third Generation in an Offspring's Household: Widows are more likely than widowers to live with an offspring, and they are more likely to live with a daughter than a son.

Sex and Aging: Recent research has revealed that both sexual interest and activity can continue into the 90s.

Living Together: Loneliness, need for the opposite sex, and financial problems often lead couples to live together without marriage.

Retirement Communities: A large apartment house or a development of single houses, built most often in warmer sections of the nation for the relatively affluent elderly.

Nursing Homes: Institutions for the aged which are generally hospital-like in their atmosphere.

Facing Death: Life-extending procedures often prolong life beyond a point where the dying or their relatives can cope with the experience.

LEARNING OBJECTIVES

Fill in the words required to complete each sentence.

Learning Objective 1

Describe the extent of widowhood in the United States.

a. Of the _____ million people in the United States who are over 65,
    _____ of the women and _____ of the men have lost their marital
    partners.

b. Most of the widowed are _____, and there are over _____ million
    widows in the United States.

c. There are about _____ times as many widows as _____.

d. There are only _____ men over 65 years of age for every 100 older
    _____.

e. More than _____ percent of older men are still married but only
    _____ percent of older women are still married.

Learning Objective 2

Describe the principal adjustments to being widowed.

a. Following the loss of her life's _____, the widow may only look forward
    to her own early _____ as life may no longer seem worth living.

b. The widow's _____ is further complicated by the loss of at least some
    of her partner's retirement _____.

c. Performance of domestic tasks helps to reinstill _____ in the widow's
    life.

d. The widow is also likely to continue her significant _____ as
    _____.

e. The _____ devastation experienced by men who lose their wives is often
    complicated by extreme _____ for the role of _____.

f. Many men are almost totally _____ on their wives for even the simplest
    of _____ chores.

g. The widower's situation is further complicated by the _____ masculine
   _____.

h. Compared to widows, widowers have far greater opportunity to _____.

Learning Objective 3

Describe the widowed who live with their children.

a. Widows are more likely than _____ to move into their children's
   _____.

b. A woman and her own mother are more likely to share similar _____ and
   routines than are a woman and her mother _____.

c. When the wife _____ outside the home, the widow may be _____
   as the primary _____.

d. The husband's _____ to the presence of his mother _____ depends
   greatly on his _____ with her and with his wife.

e. Often a special kind of "_____ relationship" develops between the widow
   and her son _____.

f. The widow in her _____ home also has a special _____ role to
   play.

g. Widows who live with their families avoid both the _____ and the
   frustrations of those who attempt to resume active and _____ lives after
   their spouses have died.

Learning Objective 4

Describe sexuality and companionship among the widowed.

a. The effects of _____ on men's and women's _____ needs are poorly
   understood.

b. Many traditional views held that interest in sex at old age was somehow
   _____ and _____.

c. Recent _____ studies show that about _____ of men past the age
   of 65 and about _____ of all men continue sexual activity into their
   80s.

d. According to the Duke study, about _____ of older women are sexually _____.

e. Widowed men and women frequently _____ relationships with persons of the _____ sex whom they knew earlier in life.

f. Among the widowed, mutual _____ often leads quickly to living _____.

g. By getting _____, most women will forfeit their _____ benefits.

h. Older couples who live together frequently encounter _____ from their _____ children.

i. A financial contract may be necessary to secure the _____ acceptance of the new _____.

Learning Objective 5

Describe remarriage among the widowed.

a. Over _____ of the remarried couples had known one another before they were _____.

b. In almost _____ percent of the remarriages, the new partners were already related by _____.

c. Most widowers remarry within a year or two of the _____ of their first _____.

d. Many remarried couples had been discreet about their _____ and avoided _____ in connection with their remarriages.

e. The most frequently stated _____ for remarriage is _____.

f. Remarried couples who sought income, household help, and nursing care more than _____ had less _____ remarriages.

Learning Objective 6

Describe the characteristics of communal living among the elderly.

a. Some of the most _____ communal groups have been organized by _____ people.

b. Not all aging persons can find a person of the _____ sex with whom they can share an intimate and _____ relationship.

c. Most senior-citizen communes seem to have developed in _____ regions of
    the _____.

d. The _____, unconventionality, and rejection of the _____ ethic
    common to younger communes seldom afflict older communes.

e. Neighbors have sometimes brought _____ or police _____ against
    older communes.

f. These communes foster continued _____, they make sense economically,
    they offer some _____ care, and they provide _____.

Learning Objective 7

Describe the principal old-age facilities available to the widowed.

a. _____ communities often appeal to the relatively _____, and they
    often require investments of from $25,000 to _____.

b. Most retirement communities cater to _____ people, and _____
    people are seldom found in them.

c. Special facilities in these communities frequently include a _____ room
    for those who can't _____, and some communities also have nursing
    _____ units.

d. The prospect of _____ and _____ are deemphasized in most retire-
    ment communities.

e. Special patterns of _____ frequently develop among the elderly. For
    example, _____ may come to care for the older _____.

f. _____ homes care for those who can no longer care for _____.

g. Typically, the nursing home patient's _____ must be shared with others,
    and there are few opportunities for _____.

h. Nursing homes are where people without _____ go to await _____,
    and they offer little _____ for anything else.

Learning Objective 8

Describe the confrontation of death among the elderly.

a. By this stage of _____, most people have had _____ with death.

b. The fewer the person's meaningful _____ the greater his or her _____ to death.

c. The _____ of death in modern society makes it more difficult for people to die with _____.

d. Often the full _____ of modern medicine is used solely to preserve _____.

e. The dying also frequently encounter _____ and concealment from their physicians and _____.

f. Medical _____ need not be the same thing as mercy killing or _____.

g. The _____ person should have the _____ to state what measures will be used to preserve his or her life.

h. Death and dying may be managed best in the _____ of _____ with loved ones.

MULTIPLE CHOICE QUESTIONS

_____1. Almost _____ percent of the women over 65 have lost their marital partners.

    a. 20   c. 50
    b. 35   d. 65

_____2. In terms of numbers, there are about _____ times as many widows as widowers.

    a. two   c. four
    b. three   d. five

_____3. Which of the following provides least help to the woman in her adjustment to widowhood?

    a. release from financial obligations
    b. continuation of domestic tasks

    c.   presence of children and grandchildren
    d.   solidarity with other widows

_____4. Which of the following has <u>not</u> been identified as a major type of grandmother role?

    a.   symbolic   c.   remote
    b.   nurturing   d.   individualized

_____5. Which type of grandmothering was <u>least</u> often found by the Wisconsin researchers?

    a.   symbolic   c.   remote
    b.   nurturing   d.   individualized

_____6. Widowers tend to fare better than widows with respect to

    a.   living closer to their grandchildren.
    b.   receiving financial support from their children.
    c.   diet.
    d.   remarriage.

_____7. The most frequent pattern of the widowed living with their adult children is the

    a.   widow living with her son.
    b.   widow living with her daughter.
    c.   widower living with his daughter.
    d.   widower living with his son.

_____8. As a group, widowers

    a.   have lower death rates than married men.
    b.   have lower suicide rates than married men.
    c.   tend to be footloose and free.
    d.   experience pressure to remarry.

_____9. The widow is most likely to be acknowledged as primary homemaker when

    a.   her daughter works outside the home.
    b.   she proves she cooks and cleans better than her daughter.
    c.   she has a good relationship with her son-in-law.
    d.   she has a poor relationship with her son-in-law.

_____10. A special kind of "_____ relationship" often develops between the widow and her son-in-law in order to reduce interpersonal strain.

    a.   attraction   c.   joking
    b.   power   d.   liking

_____11. A recent Duke University study shows that about _____ of men past 65 are still sexually active.

    a. one-fifth   c. one-half
    b. one-third   d. two-thirds

_____12. The most important reason why widows are less active sexually than widowers appears to be

    a. lack of sexual desire.
    b. shortage of available partners.
    c. lack of privacy.
    d. poorer health.

_____13. When the widowed live together, the two most frequent obstacles to remarriage are

    a. financial loss and sexual incompatibility.
    b. financial loss and children's objections.
    c. sexual incompatibility and children's objections.
    d. desire to imitate the young and financial loss.

_____14. Adult children will be most likely to accept remarriage by their widowed parents if

    a. the parent is marrying a younger partner.
    b. the parent is marrying an older partner.
    c. there is a marriage contract.
    d. there is a chance of children resulting from the remarriage.

_____15. For over half of the widowed who remarry,

    a. the marriage ends in divorce.
    b. the couple knew one another before they were widowed.
    c. the husband has been widowed longer than the wife.
    d. the husband is younger than the wife.

_____16. Success of remarriage among the widowed is directly related to the extent to which the couple are seeking

    a. nursing care.   c. increased income.
    b. household help.   d. companionship.

_____17. Compared to communes of younger people, communal living among the elderly is more likely to emphasize

    a. cooperation.   c. rejection of the work ethic.
    b. unconventionality.   d. political radicalism.

____18. In which of the following old-age facilities are elderly men and women most likely to live with each other?

    a. suburban retirement communities
    b. urban apartments and condominiums
    c. nursing homes
    d. children's homes

____19. Which of the following is the <u>least</u> common complaint against nursing homes?

    a. lack of kitchen facilities
    b. lack of privacy
    c. lack of television
    d. lack of companionship

____20. In the treatment of dying relatives, increasing numbers of Americans are advocating

    a. euthanasia.
    b. mercy killing.
    c. medical restraint.
    d. extraordinary measures to prolong all signs of life.

TRUE FALSE QUESTIONS

____1. There are more than ten million widows in the United States.

____2. There are more than eight times as many widows as widowers in the United States.

____3. A recent study of grandmothering has identified four different types of grandmother roles.

____4. Widows are likely to remarry more quickly than widowers.

____5. Widows are more likely to live with a son's family than with a daughter's.

____6. The husband's response to the presence of his mother-in-law depends greatly on his relationship with his own mother.

____7. A recent Duke University study showed that about two-thirds of men past 65 are sexually active.

____8. The finding of less sexual activity among widows as compared with widowers is probably due to an absence of available partners.

____9. An older couple that lives together frequently loses financial benefits that would be available to a married couple.

____10. Over half of the remarried widowed knew each other before they were widowed.

____11. Nursing homes are for the elderly who have no other choice.

____12. Families of the dying are increasingly likely to urge physicians to perform euthanasia on their terminally ill relatives.

MATCHING

____1. widows   a. least frequent grandmother role

____2. widowers   b. widows lack partners

____3. apportioned type   c. over ten million in the United States

____4. individualized type   d. most couples acquainted before widow-hood

____5. living with children   e. for affluent couples

____6. remarriage   f. poorly prepared for role

____7. sexuality   g. offers financial advantages

____8. living together   h. most frequent grandmother role

____9. communal living   i. neighbors frequently object

____10. retirement communities   j. for elderly without choices

____11. nursing homes   k. more likely with daughter than son

ESSAY QUESTIONS

1. Many studies suggest that remarriages among the widowed are the most satisfying and stable of all marriages. Explain why this is the case and relate your answer to the specific needs that lead the widowed to remarriage.

2. Explain why gender differences in sexual activity appear to be greatest among the aged, and describe what is likely to happen to these differences in another generation or two.

3. What does the finding that more than half of remarried couples were acquainted before widowhood suggest about the process of mate selection among the aged? Compare your answer with the process of mate selection described in Chapter 6.

ANSWERS

Learning Objective 1

a. 23, one-half, one-fifth
b. women, 10
c. five, widowers
d. 69, women
e. 70, 35

Learning Objective 2

a. partner, death
b. grief, income
c. order
d. role, grandmother
e. emotional, unreadiness, widower
f. dependent, household
g. traditional, stereotype
h. remarry

Learning Objective 3

a. widowers, homes
b. values, in-law
c. works, acknowledged, housekeeper
d. adjustment, in-law, relationship
e. joking, in-law
f. daughter's grandparental
g. challenges, independent

Learning Objective 4

a. aging, sexual
b. unclean, immoral
c. longitudinal, two-thirds, one-fifth
d. one-fifth, active
e. renew, opposite
f. attraction, together
g. married, widow's
h. resistance, adult
i. children's, marriage

Learning Objective 5

a. one-half, widowed
b. 10, marriage
c. death, wives
d. courtships, ceremony
e. reason, companionship
f. companionship, satisfactory

Learning Objective 6

a. successful, older
b. opposite, exclusive
c. warmer, country
d. competition, work
e. legal, action
f. independence, physical, companionship

Learning Objective 7

a. reitrement, affluent, $50,000
b. married, single
c. dining, cook, home
d. death, illness
e. care, widows, widowers
f. nursing, themselves
g. room, privacy
h. alternatives, death, opportunity

Learning Objective 8

a. life, experience
b. relationships, resignation
c. depersonalization, dignity
d. technology, life
e. deceit, families
f. restraint, euthanasia
g. dying, right
h. privacy, relationships

MULTIPLE CHOICE QUESTIONS

1.	c	11.	d
2.	d	12.	b
3.	a	13.	b
4.	b	14.	c
5.	d	15.	b
6.	d	16.	d
7.	b	17.	a
8.	d	18.	a
9.	a	19.	c
10.	c	20.	c

TRUE FALSE QUESTIONS

1.	T	7.	T
2.	F	8.	T
3.	T	9.	F
4.	F	10.	T
5.	F	11.	T
6.	F	12.	F

MATCHING

1.	c	7.	b
2.	f	8.	g
3.	h	9.	i
4.	a	10.	e
5.	k	11.	j
6.	d